THE VOICE OF THE PEOPLE

THE
VOICE
OF THE
PEOPLE

A CONSTITUTION FOR TOMORROW

Robert Alexander

Weidenfeld & Nicolson
LONDON

First published in Great Britain in 1997 by
Weidenfeld & Nicolson

A catalogue reference is available from the British Library

ISBN 0 297 84109 2

Typeset by Selwood Systems, Midsomer Norton
Printed in Great Britain by Butler & Tanner Ltd, Frome and London

Weidenfeld & Nicolson

The Orion Publishing Group Ltd
Orion House
5 Upper Saint Martin's Lane
London, WC2H 9EA

CONTENTS

PREFACE

Out of the crooked timber of humanity no straight thing was
ever made.

(Immanuel Kant)

The drumbeats are sounding for constitutional reform.
There is an increasingly strong belief that radical
change is needed to meet the challenges of the next
century. No constitution can be allowed to be rigidly set in
the stone of a past age. But the task of reform is delicate and
carries a high responsibility to future generations. There is no
room for opportunism or gimmickry or rushed decisions.
Ideas need to be tested against a backcloth of principle, of
experience and of realism. Nor should any single change be
seen in isolation but rather against the tapestry of our existing
constitution, the fabric of society, and the wishes of our
people.

The banner of constitutional change has generally been
carried by opposition parties. Once in government, those very
same parties have in the past become almost immediately less
enthusiastic to promote any change which reduces their own
power. They have turned conservationist, and defenders of
the status quo. This time it all seems very different. The
Labour government, elected in May 1997 with an overwhelming majority, has made constitutional reform a flagship
of its plans for government. Already it has brought in legislation to pave the way for a referendum in Scotland and
Wales, and promised to go some way towards incorporating
the European Convention on Human Rights. It has recognised
the long-standing desire of Londoners for a new strategic
authority, although confirmation of their wishes is to be

sought in a referendum. We have been promised a Freedom of Information Act, after consultation on its details through a white paper. There are pledges to improve parliamentary procedure. So it looks as if the vociferous enthusiasm of opposition will this time be translated into a much needed programme for change.

The broad thrust of this change has support going far beyond the governing party. The Liberal Democrats actively and imaginatively supported change during the long years of the last Conservative government. They are firmly on board with, and in some ways ahead of, the new government's proposals. All this should test the Conservatives in the early stages of their unfamiliar role of opposition.

The Conservative party, in spite of the economic achievements during its long spell in government, increasingly disappointed many of its supporters. It used to be the party of Europe but gradually the strident pressures of Euroscepticism have won ground and sometimes deepened into highly unattractive Europhobia. In the last few years of government, the party forsook its traditional commitments to civil liberties and introduced a raft of laws infringing what had previously been long-standing freedoms. It wrapped itself in a cocoon of blind affection for all existing forms of government and sank into a deep sleep of complacency and resistance to change. In doing so it forgot Talleyrand's famous maxim: 'The art of politics is to anticipate the inevitable and facilitate its occurrence.'

In fitting itself to lay claim to govern at some time in the future, the Conservative party should surely also help to shape the very nature of our government and promote the rights and opportunities of our people to play a full and constructive part. Our constitutional rights are precious and change should be supported by the widest possible consensus.

This book of essays does not attempt to touch on all aspects of constitutional reform. What it seeks to do is to explore the fundamental issues against which any individual proposal for change should be tested. Devolution, incorporation of the European Convention on Human Rights and the creation of a strategic authority for London do not take place in a constitutional vacuum. Each of these proposals has potentially profound significance for wider constitutional development. This is why, without delaying unduly the parliamentary processes already in train, they need mature reflection. The starting point must be an awareness and understanding of our existing rights and forms of government. What is our constitution and how much does it protect our civil liberties? What are our safeguards under the common law? Are we simply, as Lord Hailsham once said, an 'elective dictatorship' in which a powerful government can simply push any measure it likes through its tame supporters in parliament? What is the proper role of MPs, and how should they be elected? Is the House of Lords as our second chamber any real protection to us against oppressive government? What is the proper interaction between devolution and the much needed strengthening of local government? Do we need full, as opposed to partial, incorporation of the European convention if we are to be able to protect minorities and basic human rights from an over-powerful government? What should our constitutional relationship with Europe be? Do we need to have constitutional protection for the basic economic rights of the deprived and disadvantaged in our society? How should our people have their say in all these decisions? Is a vote once every five years enough? Should there be more referendums on key issues? The golden thread which underlies each of these individual issues is the need to consult, involve and respect the wishes of the people. For the touchstone of any sound constitution is whether it truly serves and protects the people.

These essays have been written over a year ending in May 1997. It was a year when proposals for constitutional reform were gaining a head of steam after twenty years of relative quiescence. During that year it had become increasingly clear that the Labour party, committed more strongly than ever before to change, would win the election. When they duly did so, they promptly introduced some of their proposals.

These essays go to print after the introduction of a bill for a referendum on devolution. By the time of publication, we will have a clearer idea of the extent to which these proposals are attracting favour. What is crucial, however, is that their long-term implications should be fully explored and understood. Every constitutional proposal must be weighed against the effect it may have on other rights and the opportunities it gives to our people to share in our government. So the aim of these essays is not to assess the current progress of the government's various individual initiatives but rather to stimulate thought about how our constitution needs to develop to meet the challenges of the next century.

In writing these essays, I am very much in debt to Mark Ashworth, a barrister and a colleague at NatWest, who has brought to our work a keen enthusiasm, a talent for research and a sensitive capacity for exploring ideas. I am also much indebted to Roger Masefield, also a barrister, who practises from my old chambers, Brick Court Chambers, for all the untiring help that he has given me over the last year. They have both helped to spark and shape some of my own thinking.

I tested out a draft of this book on some highly knowledgeable and very tolerant friends, although I remain responsible for any shortcomings. I am most grateful to Professor Jeffrey Jowell, professor of public law and vice-provost and head of the Graduate School, University College London, William Keegan, economics editor and associate editor, the *Observer*, and Anne Owers, director of JUSTICE, for giving most generously of their time and for making some very helpful suggestions. I am also grateful to Andrew Dilnot, director of the Institute of Fiscal Studies, for his thought-provoking comments on economic rights.

I am also very grateful to Jane Erith, my personal assistant. She has a spirited interest in constitutional affairs, and above all has typed and brought order to the manuscript with unfailing patience.

This is my first book. I am grateful to Lord Weidenfeld for encouraging me, as he has encouraged so many before me, to make the attempt to write even a slim volume. In doing so, it has been an education to glean a little of the contribution that is made by a skilled editor. My heartfelt thanks go to Elsbeth Lindner of Weidenfeld & Nicolson for her help and guidance.

Robert Alexander
London
June 1997

THE PEOPLE AND POWER

The art of arranging how men ought to live is even more complex than that of massacring them.
(Georges Clemenceau, Grandeur et Misère de la Victoire*)*

There is no perfect form of government, nor is there any permanent form of government. International and national dynamics, economic and social changes, unforeseen catastrophes, all continuously evolve to shape any system of government. So, too, do the needs and wishes of the groups and individuals whom democracy exists to serve. I shall not make any attempt to produce a blueprint for constitutional reform. Dogmatic, prescriptive conclusions from any individual or from any group of reformers or any single political party are simply inappropriate. It is not just for government, nor for constitutional experts, let alone for me, to impose ideas as to how the way in which we are governed should be improved. This is a task for all our people. We may all make suggestions but it is the people who should decide. Abraham Lincoln's great vision was to fashion 'government of the people, by the people, for the people'.

The phrase 'constitutional reform' has a sonorous ring suggesting that it is the priority of scholars and judges. But in truth it has a very simple aim. It is to help our society develop in a way which meets the needs of the people to whom power belongs, and for whose benefit it is exercised. Only in this way can we secure the vibrant framework needed for the stability and advance of our society.

The government of any modern country faces daunting tasks. But they are constantly changing, sometimes gradually and sometimes decisively. The controversies of one age may either die away half forgotten or become the orthodoxies of the next generation. In our own country, the extension of the franchise, votes for women, universal social security and free trade versus protectionism are all illustrations. There is now a broadly prevailing orthodoxy as to macroeconomic policy. It is recognised that there must be an underlying commitment to low inflation and that there is no long-term trade-off between inflation and high employment. This gives us a good prospect of avoiding the boom-and-bust economic cycle to which we have been so prone throughout my adult lifetime.

This encouraging prospect has been greatly reinforced by the new government's grant to the Bank of England of operational independence in the task of setting interest rates. This prompt initial act of the chancellor of the exchequer is a powerful demonstration of his commitment to sound money. We ought to be able to look forward to a much less volatile economic cycle than in the past and to solid, steady economic progress. This in turn gives individuals and businesses the priceless opportunity to plan for their futures and to flourish. The economic inheritance of the Labour government and its clear commitment to maintaining stability is a sure foundation for constructive change.

But it is only the platform, a necessary but not sufficient condition for economic and social progress. For clearly there are other striking challenges to our economy. How do we lessen the financial burdens on government and society of health, welfare and social security? How do we ensure that pensions are properly funded for the future? How do we ensure that with the apparent triumph of the capitalist free market society those who are less fortunate are not left irretrievably behind? The individual problems of the breakdown of family life, under-education, long-term unemployment, drugs and crime, and the creation of an underclass are cumulative and formidable. They are priority tasks for our society if it is to maintain and enhance our civilisation. Some might argue that compared with these demands constitutional change is simply a distraction and even an irrelevance.

Obviously these far-reaching challenges cannot be met simply by changing and altering our forms of government. Yet they cannot be met without doing so. For it is only by ensuring that the framework of government is healthy, by giving people a greater say and involving them in more decisions, that we can know their priorities and ask them to assume the mantle of responsibility and help create a holistic society. Only in this way can we lessen much of the prevailing apathy and cynicism about politics. So government by the people is not a revolutionary cry of desperation. It is undoubtedly an attractive rallying call, but it is also fundamental to the evolution of a mature democracy. After all, the Greek *Demo-kratia* meant 'people power'.

I regard it as fundamental to good government that people should be enabled to participate in taking decisions which affect their lives. Clearly this is not the only important constitutional doctrine. Accountability, responsiveness, effectiveness and equity are all vital to a healthy society. But all these important principles are firmly underpinned if people are enabled to share more in the workings of government. As George Soros, whose financial muscle in the global markets contributed to our forced exit from the Exchange Rate Mechanism in 1992, has written: 'The concept of the open society needs to be more firmly grounded. There has to be a commitment to the open society because it is the right form of social organisation.' An open society involves both improvement of communication by government and greater freedom of information available to our citizens. At one level people need access to information about themselves, to their personal files on tax, social security, police records or information about their pensions. At another level they need to be communicated with coherently and in a way which gives them access to the facts which they need if they are to participate in government in an informed way. Above all an open society means that people have a proper opportunity to have their voices heard at national and local levels on the issues which affect their lives.

But simply to recite the mantra that government should be by the people is not enough to ensure sound government. Cries for 'the people's government' can be dangerous. It was the revolution of the people which brought to power the brutal absolutism of Stalinist Russia. It was the popular vote which established the dictatorship of Hitler. To avoid the dangers of a populist dictatorship we must be vigilant to ensure that the fabric of both our constitution and our society is maintained and adapted to meet the challenges and changes of our time. Societies which either neglect or are unable to develop their constitutional structure, and which have a decaying social and economic foundation, may become the breeding ground for autocrats or even dictators. What we must continue to seek to entrench is a healthy social market democracy.

It is encouraging by contrast that democracy is gaining ground across the world, from the former Soviet Union and Eastern Europe to South America. Why has this happened? It is because alternatives have generally been corrupt and inefficient, and have often served the interests only of the rulers at the expense of the broad mass of people. The priceless gift of democracy is to enable people to have a voice in their affairs and generally political democracy paves the way for social progress. For in a democracy politicians have to seek to improve the lot of the people because they have the salutary discipline of needing their votes. If they do not meet the wishes of the people, they can be sent packing.

What are the principles that such politicians should respect and deploy? To my mind there must be two rocks on which a healthy democracy is built. The first is a consciousness that the role of any state should be limited. The function of central government should be, and should only be, to create a healthy framework for economic and social activity. It should do centrally and directly only what cannot be done more locally to protect and improve the lives of people. The baton of government should be passed down to the lowest level at which it can effectively be carried. This is, in the now familiar jargon, the subsidiarity we in this country seek from the European Union. It is also common sense, and it is the principle on which we should surely act at home. Subsidiarity is vital both to the European lexicon and to a healthy society in our own country. Limited government is also part of our bulwark against popular tyranny, and is important to preserving freedom. Large government conflicts with freedom, and it matters not by whose hands excessive powers are wielded. The elected tyrannies of Napoleon and Hitler were no more, and probably less, free than the monarchical absolutisms of Louis XIV or Frederick the Great. Nor did either of those monarchs leave the societies they controlled defeated or in ruins or, indeed, squander in vainglorious wars quite so many millions of the lives they were supposed to protect. Only if we remember the principle of continually questioning the grant of power to government will we properly serve the individuals whose interests are at the heart of true democracy.

The second rock on which a healthy democracy is built is the involvement of those individuals as much as possible in their own affairs and in the taking of decisions which affect them. The opportunity for participation must be real. People often feel helpless to influence the remote power operating from Westminster. Helplessness breeds alienation and impotence, and both breed indifference to the political process and irresponsibility on the part of the individual citizen. The power to take part in major decisions which affect us is a basic freedom. Governments say that this freedom is exercised when, from time to time, the people have an opportunity at general elections to voice their wish for change. Not only is this opportunity infrequent, but it involves accepting one party manifesto or another without the opportunity of expressing a view on individual issues.

Nor does a general election promote a deep debate of the issues. As we have seen all too recently, much campaigning is negative, and of a 'play-the-man-not-the-ball' variety. This reflects the way politicians have all too often tended to insult the intelligence of the electorate. Complex issues are traduced in strident soundbites and selective use of the facts. The people deserve a better chance to think, to test the arguments and to analyse them. The notorious man on the Clapham omnibus has a brain.

But in any event general elections are often little more than a vote of confidence on the work of the last government. The recent general election did not reflect an obvious judgement of the people on the economy, on Europe, on education policies or on wide-ranging constitutional change. What the electorate decided was that they were overwhelmingly disillusioned with the Conservative party and that the new Labour party was worth giving a chance. But should this occasional chance to overthrow the existing regime be the sole opportunity that people have to decide how they are to be governed? Why should they not have a greater voice on specific issues? Why should they have to swallow manifestos whole? Why should they not give their voice on important decisions which are taken between elections? We should surely take the chance to continue the great but incomplete advance in democracy which came with the universal franchise.

That advance was arguably the most important development for most of the people of our country in this millennium. For most of that time the great mass of people had no rights except those which government, whether monarchy or oligarchy, enlightened or unenlightened, chose to grant them. Their only voice was through angry demonstrations which risked brutal reprisals, whether in the fourteenth-century Peasants' Revolt or in the early-nineteenth-century massacre at Peterloo. But the right to vote, priceless as it is, is only an occasional and fragile involvement in government. It is the right to mount the barricades from time to time, and to hurl missiles which dislodge the party in power. That the missile is a vote, not a rock or bullet, is a great advance. Yet after voting people are left standing wondering in the dawn, waiting to see whether the new government is better or worse. It is surely time that we trusted our people more. We should allow them over and beyond the barricades and seek their greater participation in the great and lesser decisions of our times. Not only would this be fair, not only would it buttress social cohesion and sensitive government, but it could have another priceless advantage. Drawing in more of the talents of more of our people more of the time would lead to better government.

Yet, for all the need for people power, we cannot be starry-eyed that it would always be wisely or fairly exercised. Demagoguery could put that at risk. Promises of bread and circuses can sometimes have a sweeping popularity. Society needs checks and balances. So the power of the people cannot be granted without at least some minimum restraint. History shows that we must always protect people against irrational, hasty, fearful or rank populism.

Government of the people must respect all the people and not just the dominant racial or social majority. Religious and ethnic minorities, social groupings however eccentric they seem to others, individuals and families must all be respected. We must heed J. S. Mill's warning to beware of the tyranny of the majority. Here there is a role for judges. As John Marshall, an early chief justice of the United States and possibly the greatest constitutional lawyer in Anglo-Saxon history, wrote: 'The many, as often as the few, can abuse power, and trample on the weak, without perceiving that they are tyrants.' We need a framework of basic or fundamental rights which can stand as a sea wall against the strong tides of strident or extreme populism. Our society badly needs a bill of rights. At present minorities are vulnerable to the so-called sovereignty of parliament, the rubric recited by elected governments which control that parliament or by some members who, uncertain of their influence, seek to overstate the contemporary importance of the proud institutions of which they are part.

There is little novel about the aim of limiting the role of the state. Most people would regard the role of government as to perform those tasks which can only be sensibly discharged by the state on behalf of the people as a whole, and to shape and ensure a framework within which individuals and organisations are free to pursue their own goals. This definition reflects an eighteenth-century notion of freedom, all the more remarkable since it long preceded universal democracy. But the application of the principles over the years has ebbed and flowed between what has been described as maximalist government on the one hand and minimalist on the other. We have travelled from the *laissez-faire* philosophy of much of the Victorian era to the goal of socialisation of the means of production and distribution which followed the Second World War. More recently we have seen an emphasis on capitalism and privatisation of state-run industries.

But government can never withdraw too far in a modern society. Capitalism cannot be allowed to be red in tooth and claw. A limited but nonetheless vigorous interventionism is needed to protect the individual. Whether it is in the regulation of the public utilities, or the insistence on transparency of charging policies from banks, or the protection necessary for those who purchase investments with their savings, the state has devised safeguards against the deregulated society which it has created over the last twenty years. There is, too, a clearly necessary role for government in providing the social backcloth against which individuals can pursue their activities. Not just law and order, but education, health, the protection and improvement of the environment, employment policies, provision for the unemployed, the disadvantaged and the deprived, are all roles of the modern state. They cannot simply be discharged managerially. They call for value judgements and choices between competing interests and as to the relative importance of individual issues. So the role of the state is bound to remain a very important one. But the underlying principle is clear, flint-like and unchanging. Government should act only where it is necessary or highly desirable in the best interests of society for it to do so. It should create wherever possible the framework within which individuals can live their lives, help to maximise their opportunity to do so, but be alert to ensure that individuals have the freedom to pursue their goals and interests and the incentive to do so.

For the central principle of democracy is that people should be able to influence government decisions taken on their behalf. How should they have their say? What part should they play in decisions which, near to home, affect their everyday lives? Such questions can never be answered for all time. Changes in education, attitudes, aspirations, the nature of the challenges, and the role of the state mean that the tide can never be still. The process of shaping, defining and exercising democratic power must be a rolling one.

In the last seventy years the waters have remained peaceful: occasionally stirred but not shaken. Indeed, except for the reduction of the voting age to eighteen, there has been no significant formal change to the democratic rights of the people since 1928. These rights are simple but modest: to vote in general elections, normally held once every four or five years, and in local elections once every four, together with rare and isolated opportunities to express views on specific topics in referendums. In between these sporadic opportunities, governments with a large majority can do largely as they will and assert confidently, but without a sure foundation, that they are meeting the wishes of the people. Yet very often they are being driven by the media, or by a pressure group, or by skilful lobbying. Opinion polls can be some guide to what people think, but on individual issues they are sporadic and the views expressed are snap opinions offered without democratic debate. The sterile idea, sometimes trotted out by governments, that once elected they have a mandate from the people for whatever they do only reinforces the impression that people have too little say in the decisions which affect them. It enhances the perception that the political process is alien, which in turn fuels lack of understanding of great issues and an unhealthy apathy.

Yet during the seventy years since the establishment of universal franchise, the changes in society have been profound. We have been through nationalisation and then through a largely completed programme of privatisation. We have seen the extension of education and the introduction of the comprehensive system; the deepening and broadening of the welfare state; the clipping of the wings of trades unions; and laws to ensure equal opportunities for the sexes and between the races. In the wake of the Second World War socialism achieved a vogue which shaped the political consensus for the next thirty years. There followed the renaissance of entrepreneurial capitalism in the last government. Much of this philosophy has been adopted by the new Labour party. It is sometimes said that socialism has lost and that capitalism has won. If so, this leaves the profound and uneasy issue as to which party is best going to champion the disenchanted minority. Far from bringing greater equality, change and the general growth of economic prosperity have merely bred an increasing gulf and inequality within society. These are profound issues for the future and must colour the protections which need to be offered by our constitution.

So society has changed, and changed radically. But for the people to have a genuine say in their government two things are necessary: first they must have access to the information and decisions that concern them; and secondly they need a channel for communication and an opportunity for their voices to be heard. Both these aims are most easily realised in a society where power is efficiently devolved. It is only by bringing government close to the people that the people can be brought close to government.

To accept this principle is to underscore the case for change. We live at present in the most centralised state in Western Europe. During the last twenty years central government became ever more powerful. Local government was largely emasculated. The Greater London Council was abolished, leaving one of the world's largest and greatest cities without any democratic authority to co-ordinate education, environmental and planning issues, or to control to air pollution. This was consistently contrary to the wishes of the great majority of Londoners. Now the new government has rightly pledged to give Londoners a strategic authority and an elected mayor if this is what they want.

Yet the actions of the last government cannot be characterised as simply a process of centralisation. For in other areas it hived off some of its own powers as well as some of those of local government. It contracted powers out to other agencies, so delegating some of its traditional responsibility and maintaining only a policy and oversight role. Prisons were one controversial example of this trend. The regulation of schools and hospitals was effectively taken out of local political control. The aim was to secure more involvement of those who have managerial skills. Market disciplines were put in to encourage responsiveness to consumers, such as parents and patients. The Citizens' Charter was designed to stimulate increased responsiveness from public services. The aim of these changes was to give the public a better service, one more sensitive to its needs and wishes. But, however laudable these aims, it meant that managers were appointed by central government. The local people had no say in their choice. The effect of all these changes was undoubtedly to diminish local democratically exercised power and accountability. There are now about 20,000 members of non-elected bodies administering institutions which are fundamental to the well-being of people and communities.

Ultimate accountability for these activities is now with central government far away in Whitehall. This is why the health or education secretaries are heard so regularly on morning radio commenting on apparent failures in hospitals or schools far from London and of which they lack the priceless asset of some direct knowledge. This is in complete conflict with subsidiarity and is centralism absurdly over-blown. Yet increasingly the real power of the people is now limited to a twice-a-decade decision whether to keep or kick out the incumbent government. Is this sufficient opportunity for the people to participate?

In Chapter Seven I argue strongly for more powerful local government. This would complete the unfinished revolution of the last two decades. Local services are now more effectively and efficiently provided. Most local citizens are now getting better value and there is an ethos which, in the commercial world, we would refer to as customer care. But alongside this there has been a move away from local autonomy and control over services, and there are backwaters of hopelessness. The better-off now have better local schools, in part because of their greater role and influence in those same schools. But the schools in more disadvantaged areas do not have this support, and the power of local politicians to influence developments in these areas has been reduced. We are in danger of having areas of our society where there is no one to speak for and take a care for those in most need. Managerial responsiveness is vital, but so is local political accountability.

One undoubted and very powerful argument for increased involvement of the people is the steadily growing education, awareness and sophistication of the electorate. The extension of the voting franchise through the nineteenth century was slow. This in part reflected a belief that the vote should be granted only to those with a stake in the community and who were free from brute ignorance. So not surprisingly compulsory education preceded universal democracy. But, in the seventy years since the franchise was widened, voters have for the most part become much better educated and much better informed. In 1928 the school-leaving age was fourteen. 85 per cent of children left without any qualification. Less than 2 per cent went on to higher education. In 1996 by contrast, only 20 per cent (still too high a figure) left at sixteen without any qualification, and now about one-third (still too low) go on to higher education. Lives were often drab, a struggle for survival, and real opportunity was pitifully small. Desperate and poignant reminders of this leap out from the pages of polemical novels such as Walter Greenwood's *Love on the Dole* and Robert Tressell's *The Ragged Trouser'd Philanthropist*. Some say that the latter book helped win the 1945 general election for Labour. George Orwell's *The Road to Wigan Pier* is a graphic reminder of the hardship when demand fell off in the coalfields and mills of Lancashire. But what all these books, and the half-forgotten novels such as *The Marsh* and *Tell England* by the prolific Ernest Raymond, show is the desperate breadline condition of the people, with limited education, where the struggle for everyday survival granted no leisure or energy for full participation in life. Obviously some people overcome these disadvantages. In the past there were groups of people in industrial areas, like the Welsh valleys or my native Potteries, who were deeply interested in political and social issues and involved in their communities. But for the most part people lacked the time or means of knowledge to look beyond the draining demands of survival. One of the triumphs of our turbulent century has been the extent to which all this has changed beyond recognition, and at a speed of advance unparalleled in human history. Travel, radio and television, telecommunications and opportunities for leisure pursuits have all now enhanced people's horizons and choices and transformed most lives unrecognisably for the better. The silicon revolution and access to the information superhighway is further transforming the type of society in which people live. But, for all that, the say of people in the way they are governed has not been a whit increased.

What has increased, by sharp contrast, is the influence and reach of government over their lives. The historian A. J. P. Taylor has said: 'Until August 1914 a sensible, law-abiding Englishman could pass through life and hardly notice the existence of the state, beyond the Post Office and the police- man.' In 1928, when the universal franchise finally came, central government took around 15 per cent of GDP. Now it takes 40 per cent, an even more impressive difference when we remember that there has been real growth in GDP of 300 per cent. The average income per head of total population in 1928 (in today's prices) was £3,224 and the average income tax burden £174. The comparable figures for 1996 were £11,400 and £1,168. Not only does the state spend far more of our national income than once it did but there has been a steadily growing raft of controls over issues great and small – from planning, control of the environment, traffic laws, unfair dismissal and redundancy, and regulation of investments, to the control of dangerous dogs in public places and the banning of handguns. Government intervention penetrates deep into almost all aspects of our lives.

So on the one hand the voters are better educated, and on the other they are more profoundly affected by what their government does. Either of these immense changes would argue for a greater opportunity to participate in government. Together they make a formidable case that the lack of any change in the people's role in government creates an increas- ingly yawning democratic deficit.

Any doubts about this would surely be resolved by perhaps the most disturbing change of all. This is the diminished percentage of votes which has become necessary to elect a government. In the past the exercise of the universal franchise occasionally resulted in the election of governments with more than 50 per cent of the vote. But no winning party since 1935 has been supported by more than half of those who voted. Clement Attlee won a majority of more than 140 for Labour with 48 per cent of the vote in 1945.

In 1983, with 43.5 per cent of the vote, the Conservatives, led by Mrs Thatcher, gained over 60 per cent of the seats. Similarly in 1987 they had almost the same percentage of seats with some 42 per cent of the vote. Minority parties do badly in our system. In 1983 and 1987 approximately 25 per cent of the voters chose the Liberal and Social Democrat Alliance but they gained less than 4 per cent of seats. In the 1997 general election the Labour party secured 419 MPs, their largest number ever. Yet they did so on 44 per cent of the vote, in a result strongly influenced by tactical voting intended to drive out the Conservatives. They secured their record majority with a marginally lower percentage of the vote than Harold Wilson received in 1964 when he just won the election with a majority of four. It is hard to say that any of these results reflected the true will of the people. A minority vote can, through the distortions of our systems, confer a strong or indeed overwhelming parliamentary mandate. Can we do better? Would proportional representation be fairer? I believe that this should be at the heart of any constitutional debate. It cannot be right that we should have for all time an effectively all-powerful central government backed by a docile parliamentary party but elected by a minority of our people. Unless we face this challenge, constitutional change will be built on foundations of sand.

Nor can we any longer take comfort from the historical role of parliament as a brake on government. Edmund Burke stated the great proposition that a member, once elected, was not simply a representative of his constituents but should act according to his judgement and conscience. This independence of members endured for a long time. George Canning, as a young aspirant politician, eventually himself briefly to become prime minister, told William Pitt at the height of his power that he would support him provided he was free to make up his own mind on issues not of major importance to the government. Pitt responded with understanding, asking for no more than 'a general good disposition towards the government'. Through the nineteenth century and beyond, legislators not infrequently rejected the proposals of the government which commanded a majority. Groupings were less stereotyped, and more fissile, as prime ministers from Peel to Gladstone were to know.

This independence of a bygone age is now virtually dead and buried. Except when the position of the political parties is finely balanced, the government can be sure of the passage of its legislation. The House of Lords provides a wobbly windbreak against the force of strong government. The powers it has are limited, and its lack of electoral legitimacy makes it chary of exercising those powers to the full. In 1988, the attempt of Lord Chelwood, a Conservative back-bencher, to soften the inequities of the poll tax was met by a government three-line whip hailing 'backwoodsmen' from across the land to defeat the amendment. Yet within two years Mrs Thatcher was to fall, in large part through this mistaken measure and regressive tax. It was promptly and enthusiastically reversed, mainly by the surviving members of the cabinet who had helped vote it through. Parliament had failed to put a brake on the executive even where many thought it was in danger of going off the rails. The whip system and the 'rubber-stamp' philosophy were too strongly embedded. When the error was acknowledged, the very same parliament marched just as unquestioningly down the hill as it had slogged up it.

So what we have is a powerful central government, largely uncontrolled by the legislature, which permeates all areas of life and which our increasingly knowledgeable people have a very limited opportunity to influence. It is not surprising that there is a following wind for constitutional change. But the present proposals, like their predecessors twenty years ago, take the issues piecemeal. Fashionable causes, like reform of the House of Lords or devolution, dominate the agenda. Yet, to be sound and enduring, change needs to be based on principle. The debate should surely start by examining what sort of constitution we have, where power lies, whether it is adequately controlled, and whether the people should have a more effective say in the decisions taken in their name.

Between elections governments tend to want to get on with the job, speaking to, or even at, the people and not seeking their direct participation. The present government is committed to a different approach. Some Conservatives also apparently recognise that this is needed. William Hague, then secretary of state for Wales, said in early 1997: 'People in Wales, like people everywhere, want more control over their own lives.'

So indeed they do, and that is why the branches of our government cannot be left to wither and decay on their nineteenth- and early-twentieth-century roots. Our democracy needs updating. The increase in government power, the increased education of the voters, modern communications and above all the lack of effective legislative control of what are often governments with large majorities elected by a minority of the people raise again four-square the issue: what should be the rights, participation and power of the people in a healthy democracy?

CHAPTER ONE

OUR CONSTITUTION

Some men look at constitutions with sanctimonious reverence and deem them like the ark of the covenant, too sacred to be touched. They ascribe to the men of the preceding age a wisdom more than human, and suppose what they did to be beyond amendment.... Laws and institutions must go hand in hand with the progress of the human mind.... As new discoveries are made, new truths disclosed, and manners and opinions change ... institutions must advance also, and keep pace with the times.

(Thomas Jefferson in a letter to Samuel Kercheval, 1816)

What is our constitution, what is it for, and how well does it serve us? Constitutions underpin society, so it is not surprising that almost all modern states have a full written constitution. Only the United Kingdom and Israel are exceptions, although now Israel has two Basic Laws, one on Human Dignity and Liberty, and one on Freedom of Occupation. New Zealand, which until recently was another rare exception, adopted a written constitution in 1986. The British constitution has never been set out in written form, but this does not mean that we lack laws and conventions of real constitutional significance. What it does mean is that our constitution is not a coherent whole, that our fundamental rights are not clearly labelled as such, and that they are not entrenched.

Alexis de Tocqueville, in *Democracy in America*, wrote of the United Kingdom constitution simply that: 'Il n'existe point.' In this he was wrong. Constitutions do not have to be gathered together in one document. Nor are even the most sophisticated written constitutions exhaustive, providing in every way for the government of a country. Yet where there is no written constitution at all it is harder to recognise which laws are of vital significance and which have lesser status. For a constitution is the system or body of fundamental principles according to which a nation, state or body politic is constituted and governed. There would be no argument that some of our laws have just this status, whether it be legislation governing the length of a parliamentary term or providing for entry to the European Union. But in many areas the position is unclear. What some would regard as constitutional, others would describe as no more than ordinary laws. The rocks on which our citizens should be able safely to set their feet are dangerously slippery.

Some may ask why a constitution matters anyway. Most people would see a whole range of more immediate issues as far more important to their everyday lives; the economy, job creation, education, the environment, health care, provision for old age, would all come high on the list of more immediate and cogent concerns. By contrast constitutions can seem more abstract and esoteric. They deal apparently grandiosely and in legal language with the framework of government. True it is that many of them extend to a bill of individual rights, but it is rare that these seem to impinge obviously and immediately on people's lives. Nor have politicians in the past been consistent about the importance of constitutional rights. The current government has given clear recognition that constitutions are vital bulwarks of our freedom. They stake out where the institutions of the state stand in relation to us all. Our laws, our economic development and the cauldron of political activity can work properly only if constitutional boundaries are in place, well recognised and respected. Only if citizens have a proper opportunity to participate in government at all levels can their needs and wishes be recognised and met. The shape of government, central and local, crucially affects the vibrancy and vitality of our society.

But does it then follow that such a constitution must be in writing? Does a written formula help to ensure sounder and more efficient government? Is it really a protection for citizens? It can be said convincingly that the United Kingdom is among the most civilised countries in the world, and that we have not, over the years, been worse or less fairly or decently governed for want of a written constitution. It is undoubtedly true that written constitutional settlements can influence, frame, buttress and even entrench forms of governments and underscore freedoms. They may be essential to the creation of a nation. In the United States or Canada or Australia or modern Germany, the creation of a federation necessarily meant that there had to be a written separation of powers between the federal government and the individual constituent territories. Only in this way could the division of powers between central state or provincial governments be established. Written constitutions, too, were also inevitable to the creation of new countries from the colonies of the former British empire. Without them the lack of a history of self-government would have meant that there was simply a constitutional vacuum.

Our constitutional history is different. It has developed piecemeal, through the individual chapters of our history. Changes have been evolutionary and not revolutionary, and have been designed to address particular issues and problems in a pragmatic way. Our common law has developed in the same way – with changes being made singly and cautiously to deal with the important social and political issues of the day. We have not since the seventeenth century suffered the cataclysmic events which might provide the impetus for going back to the drawing board and creating an entrenched political constitution. Some argue that we should do so anyway so as to modernise comprehensively our system of government.

We should recognise that written constitutions do have considerable advantages. They can ensure that there is a clear division of powers between central and local government. The Tenth Amendment to the US constitution stipulates, with a total clarity which would be helpful for the European Union, that all powers not expressly delegated to the federal government are reserved for the individual state. Such constitutions can entrench rights, so protecting society against alarmist or suddenly populist change. They can protect minorities, and they can guard against the over-strong hand of a government elected by a minority of voters. Written constitutions can also have the real advantage of making plain for a country, which of its rights are so precious as to be regarded as 'constitutional' and which have only lesser status. This is a protection against a government tampering at a stroke, or through progressive erosion, with our fundamental liberties. It also means that, as in the United States and Germany, there is a court which can uphold constitutional rights against the legislature. We have here no such sea wall against oppression by a majority or the intolerable intrusion of an authoritarian central government backed by a strong majority in parliament. It is now rare for countries to lack, as we do, a constitutional court, thus leaving the citizens defenceless against a government which abuses basic rights.

The adoption of a written constitution can also rekindle awareness of liberties. The recent history of Canada is a striking example of a state which rediscovered its constitution. The original constitution was largely a dead letter, rarely invoked or litigated. The decision was taken to adopt a new charter, as an act of political choice and not because of political upheaval. There was a lengthy consultation exercise at all levels of society. Not only did this help to define the proposed changes. More importantly it created a strong feeling of ownership among people once the charter was adopted. It is now invoked regularly, among civil servants, politicians and groups outside government, as well as in court.

It is seen by many as a 'living tree' which can be reinterpreted in the light of changing views and societal changes, and can help shape government decision-making. Inevitably no one could predict how such a charter would operate in practice. But recent Canadian history illustrates how it can contribute strikingly to a recognition of the importance of constitutional principles and to the shaping of society.

Yet for all these advantages there is no guarantee that written constitutions will achieve these ends, and they are far from a panacea for good government. They can sometimes be a pious and cynical farce. The Soviet Union, and its satellites, had written constitutions which were operated in a way totally inconsistent with individual liberties. Nor can the finest written constitution prevent tyranny. Hitler came to power democratically, elected under the new-model Weimar constitution, and his initial predatory invasions and subsequent war were supported by most of his people. No wonder that in 1943, as the US fought for decency and the rule of law, one of their great judges, Justice Learned Hand, reminded us that: 'Liberty lives in the hearts and minds of men. Where it dies then no constitution, no laws can save it.'

Nor do written constitutions automatically ensure stability. In the century from the start of the revolution in 1789, France had no fewer than nine constitutions to shore up successive virtual despotisms. At least three of the changes were accompanied by the discordant music of shoot-outs over the barricades. Written constitutions, too, are set in the cement of the philosophy, values and conditions which give them birth. It is true that the United States' constitution has been dynamised by the Supreme Court to address issues such as education, abortion and equal rights which George Washington, Alexander Hamilton and the other founding fathers could never have guessed at. But neither the framing of the constitution, nor indeed its interpretation by the courts, could erase the blot of slavery until after a civil war of previously unrivalled carnage. Even now constitutional rights act from time to time as a drag on the development of United States law, inhibiting attempted restraints on pornography and the control of the carrying of arms. Either written constitutions have to be interpreted controversially to deal with situations that they never envisaged, or they are an unnavigable rock on which the changed conditions of life and modern society ultimately founder. Nor can written constitutions, as the small number of amendments to the American and Australian constitutions demonstrate, easily be altered. This is precisely because they are entrenched, requiring more than simply a legislative majority for change. Entrenchment of rights is a mixed blessing.

So written constitutions offer no automatic guarantee for democracy and freedom. To say that the United Kingdom does not need a written constitution such as we insisted on when granting independence to former colonies is not to argue loftily that there should be 'unequal laws for lesser lands'. It is simply to recognise our history and how our society has evolved. Our rights have been gained by a process of accretion over almost eight centuries, either by legislation or by unofficial rules which became accepted through usage and are now labelled as 'conventions'. They cover almost all the ground which is generally found in written constitutions. The role of the monarchy, the powers of parliament and the split of functions between its two Houses, the length of the parliamentary term, the divisions of power between central and local government and the role of the judiciary, they are all there, many of them long established. This mix of laws and conventions is for us the fundamental framework of our government.

If the United Kingdom were now to adopt a written constitution, it would be a leap into the unknown. No one could predict the consequences, the judicial interpretation or its long-term influence. The one attempt to introduce a written constitution in England, Oliver Cromwell's pioneering Instrument of Government, heralded the installation of an absolute dictatorship in the space of a mere decade. Indeed, the gradual slide towards anarchy that was precipitated by Cromwell's death was halted only by the nobility's decision to revert to the old model and restore the unwritten constitutional framework of the monarchy and parliament. This is surely a salutary reminder against too much radicalism. Evolutionary rather than revolutionary change has been the watch-word of the United Kingdom's constitution. So it should be in the future. The present constitutional institutions and systems have not been built overnight.

We should not, however, be too self-congratulatory over how our constitutional framework developed. We cannot pretend that it was always inspired by lofty principles or high-mindedness. Magna Carta, the much vaunted foundation of our freedoms, reflected a crude power struggle between king and nobility. The Bill of Rights of 1689 was concerned to promote the welfare of landed gentry and of merchants. The vast mass of the population gained not at all. The slow, century-long move towards the universal franchise which began in 1832 reflected far less the principle of equality of man than the wise recognition of the governing classes that they should share power enough to maintain societal stability. Our constitutional development has more of enlightened self-interest than a principled commitment to fundamental human rights.

But it has nonetheless, for the most part, been shot through with an underlying respect for fairness and the rule of law which was frequently well in advance of its times: for example, the creation of the right of habeas corpus, and the freeing of the slave James Somerset by the lord chief justice, Lord Mansfield, some eighty years before the United States erased the status of servitude. We take for granted an uncorrupt judiciary, a largely financially uncorrupted political system, high standards of integrity in the civil service and the over-riding commitment to the fair administration of justice. Suggestions of financial sleaze by MPs in the years leading up to the 1997 election, although on a much lesser level than in many countries, caused concern precisely because they are so alien to our traditions. Perhaps the most eloquent tributes to the strength of our institutions, and the commitment to the spirit of liberty, are both the historic stability of our society and the virtually complete lack of any strong demand for root-and-branch change.

Indeed, it is ultimately the spirit of the British peoples which may fairly be said to lie at the heart of our constitution. As Mr Gladstone observed more than a century ago, the British constitution 'presumes, more boldly than any other, the good faith of those who work it'.

But to say this is not to argue for inertia or for ossification of our forms of government. After all, two of the greatly prized strengths of our own constitutional provisions are their flexibility and capacity for sensitive evolution. These strengths will, however, erode, if we ever take a Panglossian approach, marvelling at the wonders of our system and drawing a line in the sand against change. Change was high on the agenda twenty years ago. The present government's agenda for change does not raise any new issues. A Royal Commission on the constitution recommended significant devolution in 1973. Lord Scarman, a notably libertarian judge, called grandiosely for 'a new constitutional settlement'. More specifically in 1976 Lord Hailsham, in *The Dilemma of Democracy*, which for all that has been written since remains the most powerful argument for constitutional change, forcefully argued that it was time for wider-ranging reform. He thought it necessary: 'to limit the unlimited powers of the legislature, partly by establishing a new system of checks and balances, partly by devolution, and partly by restricting the powers of parliament to infringe the rights of minorities and individuals'. He was in favour of the incorporation of the European Convention on Human Rights into our own law. He believed that we would be driven to set up subordinate legislative assemblies in Northern Ireland, Scotland and probably Wales, and in various parts of England. There was, so he thought, no alternative to an elected House of Lords, with proportional representation from very large constituencies. His agenda was laced with radicalism, and a distaste for the 'elective dictatorship' which gives the government of the day effectively unbridled, highly centralised power, against which the only belated check was to kick out the government at the next general election. In short, as he wrote: 'we need a new constitution, and like all new constitutions its terms must be reduced to writing and defined by law'.

His warnings were timely then, and are more so now. For the powers of the executive and legislature are sweeping and unchallengeable. The much prized doctrine of parliamentary supremacy means that each and every act of parliament is supreme, and can override any earlier acts. In constitutional terms, this is a matter of deep concern. It is a charter for potential absolutism. Since our constitution is unwritten, the delicate legislative framework within which it lies can be eradicated overnight. No single act is labelled as 'constitutional' so as to require special consideration before it is amended or repealed outright. The ease with which earlier legislation and convention may be swept aside can readily be seen from the Parliament Act of 1911, reforming the powers of the House of Lords, and the Defence of the Realm Act of 1914 which both passed through all their stages in parliament in a single day. More recently there was the indecently hasty, government-backed amendment, introduced as an afterthought into an otherwise well-considered bill on libel and defamation, which swept away part of the Bill of Rights of 1689 in the supposed interest of one member of parliament, Neil Hamilton. This permitted him to waive parliamentary privilege to pursue a libel action. That Nemesis struck when he dropped the action is no consolation for such a cavalier change to long-standing constitutional principle. Parliament is now scant check on the vast powers of government.

Legislation today all too often simply reflects and buttresses the power of the government of the day. There may be times when this power is less, when, as from 1992 to 1997, there is a narrow parliamentary majority. But for the most part the executive can drive all its radical measures home, as we saw in the case of reform of trades union laws, privatisation, rate capping, the community charge or poll tax, and successive restrictions on civil liberties. Nor do the powers of the government of the day stop with its dominance of parliament. For the government also has at its disposal large and uncodified powers of executive action which it can use without the need of any sanction at all from parliament. These are the old sweeping powers of the monarch, called the royal prerogative.

These powers are still massive. It is still possible for our government to go to war without any authority from parliament. International treaties can be signed without any debate in parliament. When the government signs up to regulations in Brussels, they automatically become part of our law under the European Communities Act 1972. So parliament has no say in bringing in these new European laws. Under the prerogative, too, governments can create and fund administrative bodies which have not been established or approved by parliament.

Take as one example the creation of the Criminal Injuries Compensation Board. This provided for the state to compensate victims of crimes of violence. It was an admirable concept, but it involved a sizeable budget at the expense of the tax-payer. It might have been thought to be an area which automatically called for parliamentary debate and consideration. But instead it was created following a government white paper, and then announced by the home secretary to the House of Commons in 1965.

Some twenty years later in 1988 the Criminal Justice Act sought to give the scheme a legislative foundation. It did so by cloning the non-statutory scheme, including its basis of assessing compensation. There was a standard provision in the act for the home secretary to decide when to start the operation of the new statutory scheme. But it was never brought into effect. The old scheme remained in force. In 1993, Michael Howard as home secretary decided simply to ignore the statutory scheme, which parliament had enacted, and to introduce without parliamentary consent a new prerogative scheme, radically different to the one which had recently been enacted. He did so without asking parliament to repeal the provisions it had approved in 1988, and so in effect simply by-passed the legislation. There was cogent complaint both as to the principle of ignoring parliament and as to the merits of the new scheme. In particular it would have deprived any injured person of compensation for loss of earnings, which previously had been fundamental to both the common law and the statutory scheme. Under the new scheme a young policeman with a family of four who was injured would get the same compensation as an eighty-year-old widow for an equivalent injury. Not surprisingly many considered this downright unjust.

The home secretary was presumably advised that he was acting perfectly lawfully in ignoring the clearly expressed will of parliament. When a challenge was mounted the courts were divided on the issue. In the end the judges of the House of Lords held that the new prerogative scheme could not be properly introduced, since it would conflict with the legislation which had been passed some years earlier and still lay unchallenged on the statute books. The home secretary had no discretion, so it was held, to decide to ignore this scheme and to proceed to another one. Parliament had limited his power simply to deciding when to bring the legislative scheme into force, and had not given him a wide discretion to disregard it altogether and leave it dangling irrelevantly in our law.

This botched saga is interesting for several reasons. Parliament had thought fit in 1988 to make the scheme statutory. But in 1993 the home secretary was prepared to put forward a quite different scheme under the executive power of the royal prerogative. So far as I can tell the reasons were pure convenience. It was easier to ignore the statute, leave it unrepealed and put the new scheme in place without any parliamentary input. But could it ever be right to by-pass parliament on an issue on which it had recently legislated? Should substantial money be committed to the scheme without any parliamentary sanction? All these were issues of constitutional principle but were each to be ignored until the courts imposed a check.

What is particularly interesting – and indeed startling – is that parliament itself, with the exception of one debate in the House of Lords, made no attempt to protect and guard its own legislation. It was prepared tamely to accept that it should be ignored and left to rot on the statute book. It was left to the courts to uphold the power of parliament which the legislators declined to protect for themselves. Then, and only then, was a new statutory scheme enacted and the old one repealed.

Most of the original Crown prerogative powers have now devolved to the government. What are the powers which are still personal to the sovereign? They include three rights – the right to be consulted, the right to encourage and the right to warn. Probably, as Walter Bagehot, the nineteenth-century editor of *The Economist* and constitutional writer said, 'a King of great sense and sagacity would want no others'. But there are theoretically some more extreme powers. There is the need for the sovereign to consent to all legislation. This consent was last refused by Queen Anne as long ago as 1707. The sovereign has the theoretical right to appoint and dismiss ministers. This includes the prime minister, although this power is now much less potentially important with the current procedures which exist in each party to govern the choice of a leader. But it could conceivably have some force in delicate situations if, as in 1974, no party had a clear parliamentary majority. In Australia, where there was a deadlock between the two Houses of parliament over the grant of finance to the government in 1975, the then governor-general dismissed the prime minister. Clearly, as the protest (which dogged him for the rest of his days) illustrated, and even though the dilemma he faced was peculiarly difficult, wise constitutional conventions are vital to prevent such a contretemps from arising.

As well as legislation and prerogative powers, our constitution is shaped by what are called 'conventions'. These are designed to guide the exercise of the prerogative power of government, as well as the sovereign. They provide the framework for the use of broad and sweeping executive powers. One vivid illustration is that the Australian constitution makes no mention of the office of prime minister or of cabinet government. It was taken for granted that the English model of government would be followed. In the same way, appointments, dismissals, and resignations of ministers are governed by the prevailing constitutional conventions.

What, then, are these conventions? They are a collection of customs or rules which are respected by those responsible for working the constitution but which are not strictly enforceable as rules of law. Some, such as Bagehot, have occasionally pressed for codification of the conventions. But, since they evolve and subtly change, such an exercise would become largely futile within the space of a few years. It is by convention that most of the powers of the monarch have been transferred over centuries to the elected government. How, for example, does the sovereign choose the prime minister? On the appointment of Lord Home in 1963 she took informal advice where there was no mechanism for formal choice by the Conservative party. When the system of election of the leader of the Conservative party was put in place, the convention changed smoothly so that both prime minister and sovereign respected the decision of the party. Margaret Thatcher's resignation and the appointment of John Major reflect this changed convention in action. Conventions are never written in stone and often change to reflect shifts in political realities.

There is obviously a marked, and largely advantageous, benefit in the flexibility of conventions. Since they mostly reflect current political trends and developments, they must obviously be prone to change. But the way they change is haphazard. If a constitutional convention is frequently disregarded and no objection is raised, it becomes assumed that convention has fallen into disuse, as may now be the case with the decline of the doctrine that ministers should resign in the case of serious errors by civil servants. With the devolution of government power to outside agencies, the previous government evolved the convention that ministers are responsible for the failure of 'policy' aims but not for failures of 'operational' matters. This had the effect in practice of limiting sharply the doctrine of ministerial responsibility. It is a far cry from the days when in 1981 Lord Whitelaw, as home secretary, offered his resignation because an ultimately harmless man found his way into the queen's bedroom in Buckingham Palace. Interestingly, and healthily, the new home secretary, Jack Straw, has stated that once again ministers are going to answer on issues affecting prison operations.

But, shift as they do, conventions are deeply involved at all levels of government. They regulate many of the relationships between the Houses of parliament, the roles of the civil service, the police and armed forces, the relationship between ministers and the machinery of justice, and that between the United Kingdom and other members of the Commonwealth. Which conventions can be said to be 'constitutional' and which of lesser significance? There is no clarity, and no agreement. With this lack of certainty, it is remarkable that they have operated so long in a way which has so generally carried respect and won the assent or at least the acceptance of sovereign, government and the people. It is yet another reason for being sceptical of too wide-ranging constitutional change. But, as against that, we need to be alert to know which among these conventions are true safeguards of sound democracy. Where, too, conventions subtly change, we need to have a way of knowing which changes are of constitutional significance. For unwritten conventions, changing as they do with practice, are inevitably the weakest defence of our freedoms. What is done regularly by government becomes a convention, which is no constitutional protection at all.

So our constitution is a mix of laws, prerogative and conventions. Some of these are, as all would agree, constitutional. Others are in a penumbral area, and their status is far from certain. Inevitably this means that our constitutional rights are shadowy, all too easily eroded, and they lack the priceless virtue of entrenchment against the passing fashions of populism. This protection, and the knowledge of what our constitutional rights were, would be a marked advantage of a written constitution. But, accepting that such a radical change carries its own drawbacks and is not currently in the realm of practical politics, there is no doubt of the importance of proper constitutional arrangements. They are fundamental to the maintenance of freedoms, to the participation of people in government, and to the priorities, effectiveness and sensitivity of that government. The very fragility of our constitution has its compensations if, but only if, we are alert to modernise its principles.

One most welcome and overdue reform is the proposal to incorporate the European Convention on Human Rights. I discuss this in Chapter Nine, but in essence it goes some way to requiring government to respect some of our fundamental freedoms and giving the courts power to act as a check on government. The very fragility of our basic liberties makes this a highly important development. But the convention only touches on some of our rights and liberties. How can we keep the benefits of our unwritten constitution and yet make an objective assessment of which changes to our laws are constitutional? In the absence of any written constitution, this cannot be achieved through the adoption of a supreme court, as in Germany, France or the United States. But it would be possible to have some less authoritative, yet important, governance through a constitutional commission consisting of senior members of both Houses of parliament and possibly judges and influential people drawn from across the spectrum of society. It would have the stamp of authority of a powerful government committee of both Houses of parliament and powerful outsiders. This commission could look at proposed or impending changes, whether at the instigation of the government or on its own initiative, and clearly highlight where a constitutional issue is involved. It could examine whether such reforms appear to cut across long-accumulated constitutional rights, the extent to which they do so, and, in the case of Europe, whether they are issues in relation to which the doctrine of subsidiarity should apply. Equally, such a commission could scrutinise the details of proposed devolution, and details of reform of local and central government, and highlight their consequences. It could, as later essays suggest, have a wider role, including monitoring the effect of proposed European Union legislation on our own laws, and the questions to be put in referendums. Obviously this is but one form of a monitoring organisation. The proposed Human Rights Commission could also possibly develop to fulfil at least part of this wide-ranging role. What matters is that we should have some organisation which is knowledgeable, brings in a broad mix of expertise, and can undertake the necessary background research. As the Nolan Committee has done, it would have to win respect and authority by the quality of its recommendations.

Such a body would operate as a searchlight to draw attention to potentially wide-sweeping reform of our fundamental rights and liberties as a nation. Surely our people are entitled to know, outside the polemic of party-political debate, what are the issues of genuine constitutional importance – and to get a considered and objective view on the merits of change? If, unlike Australia, they cannot simply get hold of and read their constitution, and yet the constitution is to belong to them as both their protection and their property, then people need all the help they can get to know what it embraces and when it is endangered. In a democracy people must be at the very least given the chance to participate in their affairs. To do so they need to understand, for otherwise they have no hope of playing a sensible, informed part. Without their understanding of what we mean by our constitution and what we include in it, our society is the poorer and the more fragile. As Francis Bacon said: 'In the theatre of man's life it is reserved only for God and angels to be lookers on.' A constitutional commission could help draw people in to the shaping of our government and the way it changes.

Such a commission could not give the rock-like stability of a constitutional court which could act as a bastion against an oppressive government. But without a written constitution there can be no constitutional court. The commission could, however, do much to inform people of their rights and where those rights are in danger. It could raise the flag for liberty. In a country where the executive government is backed by a strong and tame majority in parliament, and also has sweeping executive or prerogative powers which need no consent at all from parliament, such a flag is increasingly vital, and its colour would often be amber and sometimes red.

CHAPTER TWO

THE COMMON LAW

Have a care over my people. You have my people – do that
which I ought to do. They are my people. Every man oppresseth
them and spoileth them without mercy: they cannot revenge
their quarrel, nor help themselves. See unto them, see unto
them for they are my charge. I charge you even as God has
charged me.

(Queen Elizabeth I to her judges)

In the elusive search for our constitution, few writers linger
long on the role of the common law. The residual powers
of the sovereign, the extent to which the government
controls or is controlled by parliament, the strength or otherwise of constitutional conventions, our relationship with the
European Union, and the centralisation of power are all in
the powerful beam of the searchlight. But we rarely focus as
intensely on the part which the common law and judges play
in protecting our liberties. Yet it is a highly important part.
What judges can do, and what they cannot, are part of our
constitution. For example, how far is there a true separation
of powers between government and judiciary? Or are there
limitations on the powers of judges which demonstrate that
we lack the constitutional safeguards which we need against
the power of an elective dictatorship? The common law was
historically the foundation of many of our freedoms. We
cannot know how much liberty in practice is ours without
looking at our legal system and the part which our judiciary

plays in the protection and development of society.

The oldest element of our legal system is the criminal law. For more than eight centuries it has played a vital part in protecting basic human rights, such as the sanctity of life and the right to respect for property. The earliest fundamental purpose of the state, as recognised by Adam Smith, was the preservation of law and order as a framework of life for its citizens. To be effective this framework needs to be independent, to be free from corruption and to guarantee a fair trial. Since the Bill of Rights of 1689 these have been basic commitments of our legal system. They are buttressed by the right to trial by jury in serious cases, and by the banning of torture or other oppressive means of securing a confession. No one would suggest that there have not from time to time been blots on this system, or unjust convictions. But the outrage and unease when such occurrences are unearthed speak eloquently of our instinctive and long-standing commitment to these basic values.

Some of these protections for individuals, such as the rules governing the admissibility in court of evidence obtained through police questioning, are now governed by statute law. Some continue, however, to depend purely on the common, or customary, law and procedure laid down by the judges. The most notable of these is the so-called golden thread which underlies the conduct of trials, the need for the prosecution to prove its case against the accused and to do so beyond reasonable doubt. In rare cases this burden of proof has, on individual issues arising in a particular criminal offence, been reversed by legislation. For in this area, as in others, parliament has the power to change the law. Ultimately these protections of the citizen against unsafe convictions, or unfair procedures, depend in our law essentially on the instinct for fair play of governments, legislators and the judiciary. So far these have, for the most part, held good, although even the judges have occasionally wavered in times of national crisis. Indeed in the Second World War the highest court held that the power of detention granted to the home secretary under the Defence of the Realm Acts could not be reviewed. The power was above the law, however unfairly it was exercised. In later peaceful times judges have been more robust and seen this approach as an abdication by the courts of their essential task of holding the ring between the state and the citizen.

The civil law has also been a powerful way in which the common law has demonstrated its commitment to rights and freedoms. In the eighteenth century the courts refused to recognise slavery in this country, the best part of a hundred years before the same freedom was won by a bloody and divisive war in the United States. At about the same time, in a celebrated constitutional case, a plea of national interest was not allowed to undermine that solid principle that an Englishman's home is his castle, when a publisher had his house and papers ransacked by messengers sent from a secretary of state who had failed to obtain a search warrant. In the course of the eighteenth and nineteenth centuries, the law of libel developed as an attempt to balance the right of the individual to his proper reputation against the freedom of the press to publish facts which were true, to comment, and to report debates of public importance. In other cases, the right to free speech has been balanced against the right of an individual, or business, or government, to the protection of their confidential information. Cases like the *Spycatcher* affair, where the government tried to stop the publication of a former MI5 agent's memoirs, show that this is an area of the common law which is developing to reflect the limitation on the powers of national courts in an age of global and instantaneous communication. With the fast-growing use of the Internet this will be an ever-increasing challenge for all systems of national law.

Historically the civil law was comparatively limited in scope. It protected rights of contract and property. It existed principally to resolve commercial disputes and actions affecting the ownership or use of land. These were the concerns of the landed and merchant classes, and below them there were few legal rights or practical means of enforcing them. The law created individual and apparently compartmentalised causes of action, such as nuisance, trespass, assault and battery, defamation, deceit and breach of contract. From its first embryonic state the law also created the doctrine that governments and institutions must act within the powers granted to them and show some procedural fairness in their decision-taking. This doctrine is now a powerful force protecting our citizens against arbitrary or biased government. The principles on which the common law acts are flexible, and have enabled it to adapt gradually but fundamentally to meet at least some of the needs of a century of immensely rapid social and technological change.

Some of this evolution might seem to be somewhat technical law-making without any significant consequences for society at large. The common law 'broadens down from precedent to precedent' and its doctrines build up by a gradual process of accumulation. Nonetheless this process of evolution has kept pace with some of the fundamental changes of modern society. Thus since the Second World War the judges have created new forms of action to prevent what could otherwise be glaring injustice. They have fashioned a right which protects a person's confidential information where it is disclosed to someone else for a limited purpose, or falls accidentally into the hands of third parties. The judges created a right to help a deserted wife gain and protect her rights in a house registered in her husband's name. This in turn helped to fashion thinking which led to greater change by legislation. The judges broadened the range of situations where a person could be prevented from going back on a promise which did not amount to a binding contract but which had nonetheless been relied on by the person who had been given the promise. The judges also developed a law which enables courts to freeze assets which in the modern world a person being sued could otherwise easily transfer out of the jurisdiction to avoid their being seized if he loses the claim. In this way the judges have prevented claimants being left helplessly whistling for their money at the end of a successful lawsuit. They have widened the right of someone to recover money which they have paid where allowing the person to keep it would amount to an undeserved windfall gain or, as the law puts it, to unjust enrichment: for example, if someone makes a payment by mistake. These are only a few examples which show that the common law has still the vitality and ability to adapt to changing expectations and new situations.

But far more striking than these specific illustrations have been two developments of fundamental importance in the common law. The first has been the creation and extension of the law of negligence which is now at the heart of so many civil actions between individuals. The second has been the renaissance, broadening and deepening of the concept of judicial review as a check and restraint on the exercise of ever-increasing government power. These are two very different areas, yet in each of them we see the strength and dynamism of the common law pushing its frontiers forward to meet the changing challenges of our modern society.

The law of negligence reflects a simple moral right, the right to expect our neighbours to take reasonable care not to harm us. Perhaps surprisingly, until as recently as 1932 the law did not accept that this was a general right. The law protected us against assault, or nuisance from a neighbour's adjacent property, or fraud, but there was no general responsibility on any of us to behave with reasonable care towards each other. The decision which created a wider duty of care and the modern law of negligence was truly seminal, and all the more notable because it came during a time of judicial quietism which prevailed between the two world wars. A girl fell badly ill when she drank a bottle of ginger beer said to have contained the body of a decomposing snail. She had not bought the bottle herself: rather her boyfriend had. So she had no rights under a contract. But, by the narrowest of judicial majorities, and led by a celebrated judge, Lord Atkin, who generalised from the law relating to highway accidents and accidents in the workplace and on private property, the judges laid down the principle that neighbours, or those who might be affected by each other's acts, owe one another a duty of care. This obviously raised issues for future cases as to who in any given situation can in law be regarded as a 'neighbour' and what is the extent of the duty. This is a classic illustration of the way the common law works. The boundaries of the law of negligence have been worked out, although never finally, in individual cases over the last sixty-five years since the case.

The creation of the law of negligence was timely. With an increased population, with the coming of the motor car, with greater opportunity for individuals to act in a way that affected other people, some broad legal approach to individual social responsibility was surely necessary. So it is not surprising that the duty of care has been gradually extended. Originally it was limited to compensating people who had suffered physical injury. But it has developed to apply equally to forms of psychological or nervous distress. In this way some of those traumatised by the death or injury of relatives or friends in the Hillsborough football disaster recovered damages. So, too, have those who have suffered financial loss, whether as a result of injury or the negligence of accountants or Lloyd's insurers. More recently the courts were able to confirm at long last that the duty of a solicitor who draws up a will is owed not just to his client who is making a will and who has paid him for his services, but also to the intended beneficiaries of the will who in reality will suffer if the will is drafted negligently. This was a long-awaited triumph of common-sense over legal nicety. No one knows how the law of negligence will develop to apply to new situations in future. But the way it is gradually worked out and shaped inevitably and rightly reflects changes in the nature and expectations of society. It also demonstrates the ability of the common law at its best to fashion a principle and then extend its development to meet the justice of individual cases.

It would now be hard to contemplate life in our society without a sensibly developed law of negligence. But so, too, would it be almost inconceivable that we should lack a law of judicial review. This is at the heart of what is now called public law. Public law is as clear an example as we have of the principle of the separation of powers between the courts and the executive. It allows the courts to police the powers of the executive and its subsidiary quangos. The principles on which it rests can be found faintly but surely in decisions going back to the eighteenth and nineteenth centuries. Why has it blossomed only in the last fifty years? In the same way as the law of negligence, the growth of judicial review reflected changes in society, especially the increased power of government and its impact upon individuals. Stemming from the great reforming Liberal government before the First World War, and given impetus by both the two wars and universal democracy, the centralised welfare state developed and bureaucracy and government regulation mushroomed. The citizen came up against the state at every turn, in vital areas of life such as education, social security, licences to trade, housing, planning and immigration: and with this increased range of executive powers came an increased opportunity for abusing power. The inevitable response of the law was to flex and develop its muscles to resist such excesses.

Yet initially the courts were slow to respond. In the years between the two world wars the courts were reluctant to fetter the growing powers of government, and the lions of the judiciary seemed to sleep beside the throne. This continued until well after the Second World War. When I started at the Bar some three decades ago, the courts were instinctively liable to sympathise with arguments advanced by governments. The task of upsetting executive decisions was a tough one. But gradually this changed. The courts began to emphasise the extent to which the government was limited in its power of action by the strict powers which they had been granted by parliament. They also began to stress that in exercising those powers ministers and administrators should act fairly, sometimes seeking out representations and views from people potentially affected by decisions, and always taking them into account when they were made. They also emphasised that only those considerations which properly related to using a power could be taken into account. All these were traditional principles, but their prominent and regular reassertion and application have led to a developed system of administrative law. All this was much helped by an act of parliament in 1981 which cast aside old-fashioned procedural shackles by giving people a more general right to sue. The pace of change quickened, and it has gone on doing so.

There is no doubt that these developments in administrative law have made administrators and ministers nervous. While the impact of individual cases has been clearly felt, perhaps the greater effect has been on the general quality of approach to governmental decision-making. In many ways the greatest tribute to the influence of the courts was the publication of a civil service document called *The Judge over Your Shoulder*, which advised Whitehall insiders on how best to avoid getting their wrists slapped by the court by providing a check-list of procedural and substantive matters for them to consider before they made their decisions.

The greater assertion of judicial power is clearly an important constitutional shift and increasingly has been seen as carrying the risk of confrontation between the government and judiciary. In one sense it is remarkable that for some years governments have often grumbled privately about judicial decisions, but in public exercised a statesmanlike restraint. But the stakes have recently been raised. At least one individual minister in the last government not only exercised his undoubted right to appeal judicial decisions, but was also prepared to mix it publicly with attacks on the judges. By this and other comments the government gave the impression of being embattled, and the judiciary sought with some vigour to defend their legitimate constitutional territory. It is all too easy for governments to climb into a bunker and claim that the judiciary are set against them. This sensitivity is understandable: the press highlight the successful claims against government, not those which fail. But there are many restraints built into the court process. The courts investigate only the statutory powers, and the procedures adopted by decision-makers. They will not normally interfere with decisions on their merits, however strongly they may personally disagree with them. Judges can overturn a decision on its merits only if they conclude that the decision is one which no reasonable person in the position of the decision-maker could make, which means that it must be clearly perverse. So judges attempt not to usurp the role of government, but rather to confine government to its proper powers. As a matter of procedure, too, there is a filter. It is necessary (although not in Scotland) to obtain leave from a judge to start a claim and this is normally granted only if a person can show that he has a good arguable case. The workings of this barrier can be seen from the statistics. Over half the applicants for judicial review are not allowed to start their cases. Less than a third of those granted leave are ultimately successful in their claim. Or, in other words, only about 15 per cent of judicial review applications succeed.

So it is heartening that in his 1996 speech on the constitution John Major said:

> I see nothing surprising in the increasing role of judicial review. I believe it is a function of the increasing complexity of administration, and the legislation which governs it. And it is clearly right that the courts should hold ministers and departments to the proper use of their powers, and should safeguard the procedural quality of public decision-making. This is merely an example of our constitution working. But, by the same token, it is of course ultimately up to parliament to decide the

laws on which judges and courts make their judgments.

He was surely right in his view, and I hope the new government will share it. While the judges should clearly exercise their powers sensitively, and not seek out opportunities to follow their own political instincts, the fundamental basis of judicial review should be uncontroversial in a democracy which respects the rule of law. It is the duty of the courts to ensure that the government and its agencies act within, and only within, the limits of the powers given to them. Fair procedures are no more than a rational and decent society deserves. The litany of cases where the courts have protected individuals or groups against the abuse of power, whether under Labour or Conservative governments, is an eloquent indication of the extent to which judicial review is a crucial constitutional protection. The courts have been particularly alert to uphold and assert the claims of the disadvantaged, whether they be the homeless, asylum-seekers, immigrants, claimants for social security benefit or prisoners. The judges have been prepared to push back the boundaries to test whether government action was so discriminatory or outrageous as to be set aside. In the absence of the incorporation of any bill of rights, judicial review has become the most powerful constitutional remedy for our citizens. The partial incorporation of the European Convention on Human Rights will reinforce this remedy, although it will give no ultimate protection against oppressive legislation (because the promised Bill of Rights will not override other acts of parliament).

So these are important areas where the common law has kept abreast with modern times, so as to remain one fundamental source of our basic rights and freedoms. It also has some qualities that make it particularly efficient in performing that task. The common law is more malleable than statutes. Legislation must be interpreted with regard to its precise language, and there are limits to which the court can have regard to the broad spirit of the legislation or fill in legislation to cover situations the draftsman has not thought of. In contrast to this, the common law operates by way of a system of precedent: this depends on extracting principles from former cases, a process that is clearly susceptible to judicial moulding when that is thought to serve the interests of justice. The many and varied judgments of Lord Denning epitomised just this creative use of the common law. So, too, today do those of Lord Woolf.

Another advantage of the common law is that it can plug some of the gaps in our constitutional framework as and when the need arises. Legislation is often slow to arrive, and parliamentary draftsmen cannot think of everything. Given that this is so, any system of law needs to have a fall-back or safety net. The common law provides just such protection, and ensures that many gaps are filled that might otherwise deny people justice. A recent illustration was the decision of the courts to allow a tax-payer to claw back payments which turned out to have been unlawfully demanded by the government.

A further significant strength of the common law is that it develops rights and duties in real situations. The pros and cons of the alternative solutions are extensively argued. A balance can be struck between competing interests more finely than can ever be achieved in the hypothetical debates of parliament. These advantages mean that our common law is a bulwark and protection to all of us. Our judges have high integrity, ability and dedication, and have shown no temptation to interfere with the proper role of government.

So the achievements and the flexibility of the common law are very important. But these very strengths also impose limits on the extent to which it can shape society. As we have seen, the essence of the common law is that it works by establishing and applying principle in individual cases. It does not take the basic social and economic decisions which have to be made by the government of any modern state. Nor should the judges be asked to do so. It is not, and cannot properly be, the role of unelected judges to take a broad policy decision for society. This is the task of government and legislators. In the nineteenth century it was parliament, not the common law, which limited the hours of child labour, and it was parliament which brought in protection for workers against dangerous machinery. In this century it is legislation that has created what we now regard as important basic rights – to education, to social security, to state pensions, to protection against unfair dismissal and redundancy, and to protection against racial and sexual discrimination. All these call for essentially political judgments about the development of our society and its priorities which can be taken only by an elected government.

In the same way, the development of planning and environmental legislation has been almost entirely outside the ambit of the courts. The court may protect an individual right to light, or an individual right to a flow of water, and resolve disputes between neighbours, but it cannot lay down the blueprint for the development of society in these areas. Divorce laws, involving sometimes conflicting social policies, can be formed only by a government acting with the authority of parliament. Governments have stepped in to fill the gap with compensation schemes. Professor Jeffrey Jowell, in a notable recent analysis of judicial review, has stressed that the role of the judge as policy-maker is one which is constitutionally inappropriate, because in a democracy policy-making is the province of the executive or legislature. For him, too, the process of decision-taking is one for which judges are institutionally unsuited because they do not have the skills or knowledge of the competing arguments which are available to a decision-maker.

This consciousness of the role of the government in changing the law can sometimes make judges stand back where they theoretically have power to intervene. They are understandably reluctant to step into areas where it can be argued that policy decisions should be taken by the legislators. Take privacy. Over many years the common law has never quite closed the door to the possible creation of a right of privacy. The absence of such a right has given great cause for unease in recent years. There have been two enquiries conducted over the space of a few years by Sir David Calcutt QC. A former government minister said a little while ago that the press was drinking in the 'last-chance saloon'. Yet the last government was reluctant to call 'time' by legislating. Elected governments are rightly cautious about limiting the scope for press freedom in any way. Indeed they should not do so lightly, since press freedom is a vital aspect of democracy. But in any event governments are unlikely to risk invoking the wrath of the press by seeking to clip their wings.

Some senior judges have suggested that the courts still could develop a right of privacy if parliament did not do so. Lord Wilberforce, one of the greatest judges of our time, has said that 'privacy is one of those areas where it may be appropriate for the judge to take a hand'. But, in one of the most blatant cases of invasion of privacy of recent years, the courts declined to intervene. Gorden Kaye, a well-known actor, had his privacy when in hospital after an accident invaded by the press barging into his room to take photographs. There could hardly be a greater violation of what most of us would regard as an elementary right to be let alone, and at a time and place where the victim would inevitably be feeling particularly vulnerable. But the courts granted no redress. Lord Justice Bingham, now lord chief justice, said that the case:

> highlighted . . . the failure of both the common law of England and of statute to protect in an effective way the personal privacy of individual citizens. If ever a person had a right to be let alone by strangers with no public interest to pursue, it must surely be when he lay in hospital recovering from brain surgery and in no more than partial command of his faculties. It was that invasion of his privacy which underlay the plaintiff's complaint.

Yet it alone, however gross, did not entitle him to relief in English law.

By contrast the courts can show more confidence where they can attach legal protection to a right of contract. Here they are on familiar and traditional territory. They were able to recognise the validity of the claim of the Princess of Wales for invasion of privacy by the owner of a gymnasium. She had a contract of membership, with an implied right to privacy when on the health club's premises. This concentration on forms – depending on whether there is or is not a contract – neatly illustrates the way in which the common law tends to work. There is a long historical emphasis on contractual and property rights, so the courts are comfortable where they can rely on a contract to prevent breach of privacy. But it means that no broader right to privacy, independent of contract, has yet been recognised. It is surely unsatisfactory that so fundamental an issue should turn on the accident of whether or not there is a contract between two parties. The courts, despite an apparent power to shape the law, have so far stood aside from a key issue of individual rights and freedoms. They tend, in areas where parliament can act, to wait for such action.

The lack of a general right to interest on unpaid debts is another good example of the self-imposed limitation of the common law where change has long been thought desirable. The present state of the law makes no sense. If a business chasing a debt starts legal proceedings, a right to interest then dates back to the day on which payment was due. But without legal proceedings, and in the absence of a specific agreement to pay interest, there is no such right. The position is totally illogical. Why should someone who pays a commercial debt late not have to pay interest on it automatically? It is now over one hundred years since the judges in the House of Lords suggested that legislation was needed to remedy this injustice. More recently the House of Lords recognised that 'the present

49

state of the law . . . places the small creditor at a grave disadvantage vis-à-vis his substantial and influential debtor'.

But the judges could only repeat that it was for parliament to remedy this injustice in this branch of the law. Parliament was slow to rise to this challenge. The last government introduced several measures to encourage firms to pay their bills promptly, but these fell well short of a legal right to interest. Yet through and after the last recession late payment of debts was close to the top of the list of any survey of the difficulties confronting small businesses. The new Labour government has committed itself to taking this necessary and long-overdue step. But the inability of the courts to put right what they long recognised as an anomaly demonstrates the limitations of the common law.

We are overall immensely fortunate in the common law. It has provided an approach to the criminal law which is independent, uncorrupt and, despite isolated failures, scrupulous in its intent to be fair. The standards of personal integrity and ability of our judges are very high. In the area of civil law it has done a good deal to preserve the rights of individuals. Most notably it has brought into sharp relief the importance of upholding the separation of powers and confining government to its proper, authorised function which must be discharged in a way which is fair to those affected. The continued existence of the common law is an important constitutional safeguard. Judges do not, as was once suggested, simply declare the common law. A great American judge, Mr Justice Cardozo, said: 'The theory of the older writers was that judges did not legislate at all. A pre-existing rule was there, embedded, if concealed, in the body of the customary law. All that the judges did was to throw off the wrappings, and expose the statute to our view.' Justice Cardozo took the view that such a fiction could not long prevail. A later fine English judge, Lord Radcliffe, put it this way: 'There was never a more sterile controversy than that upon the question of whether a judge makes laws. Of course he does. How can he help it? . . . Judicial law is always a reinterpretation of principles in the light of new combinations of facts. . . .' Lord Reid, for so long the leading judge in the House of Lords, was even more forthright, regarding the suggestion that the judges merely declared the pre-existing law as nothing more than a 'fairy tale'.

Judges have always made the law. But even so there are many constraints. Perhaps the greatest constraint is that many of the policy issues for our society fall fairly and squarely to be decided by government. Once government have done so through parliament, it has long been the law that the judges have loyally to give effect to the legislation. Parliament remains supreme. So in effect the power of government is supreme and absolute since, as we have seen, parliament in practice almost invariably does what the government tells it to. Under the government's proposals partially to incorporate the European Convention on Human Rights, the government will still be able to introduce legislation against the protection of the convention, and the judges will be powerless to strike the legislation down.

The judges can therefore do only so much to protect our freedoms. They can use the principles of the common law to shape judicial review. They can find that the decisions of ministers are out of proportion, or discriminatory or irrational, if they infringe basic rights such as free speech or access to justice. They can force ministers to apply fair procedures in reaching their decisions. They can confine government to the use of the powers granted to them by parliament, and they can police the ways in which those powers are used. Some, notably Lord Scarman and more recently Lord Woolf, have suggested that they may even be able to go further and decline to give effect to legislation which conflicts with those freedoms which are so central and long-standing as to be regarded as part of our immutable law. But this approach, tempting as it would be in extreme situations, seems a doubtful constitutional safeguard. For there seem to be no exceptions to the view that judges must defer to the will of parliament.

Indeed it has long been the authoritative view, set out by Sir Ivor Jennings in his classic work *The Law and the Constitution*, first published in 1933, that it is parliament and not the common law which is sovereign. This has found an echo from Lord Mackay, then lord chancellor, who said in a speech in 1996:

> suggestions by some parts of the media that the judiciary is contemplating refusing to give effect to parliament's will have recently been described by Lord Wilberforce as a 'health scare, based on exploratory, extra-judicial utterances', and I strongly endorse his assessment.

So it is clear that parliament could abolish even the most cherished of our freedoms, and the judges, or those of them who did not resign, would have to give effect to the new law. The limits of the common law, and the constitutional subservience of the judges, mean that our traditional legal rights, however vigorously upheld, are no substitute for essential and entrenched constitutional protection. As Lord Reid observed:

> It is often said that it would be unconstitutional for the United Kingdom Parliament to do certain things, meaning that the moral, political and other reasons against doing them are so strong that most people would regard it as highly improper if Parliament did those things. But that does not mean that it is beyond the power of Parliament to do such things. If Parliament chose to do any of them, the courts would not hold the act of Parliament invalid.

The courts can do much. But they cannot do enough to safeguard our fundamental freedoms. They cannot ensure that parliament makes good or humane law, and they cannot stand as a rock to protect us against legislation which infringes human rights. The courts play a vital and large role in holding the ring between the state and the citizen. They can enforce proper standards of decision-making by central and local government. Yet they cannot at present compensate for the ineffectiveness of parliament, or guard us against bad or authoritarian laws. Such laws, as the last parliament showed, can erode our liberties in a way which the courts are powerless to prevent. Without a full bill of rights, our judges are helpless to protect us against oppressive or tyrannical government. In lacking this safeguard we are almost alone among civilised nations. This is why the European Convention on Human Rights should be incorporated in full into our own law to give the courts power to protect us against the risk that a government may in the future force legislation through parliament which conflicts with our basic rights. The current proposals of the Labour government as discussed in Chapter Nine will not give us this full protection. Only if judges can strike down laws which infringe basic human rights will our citizens have the constitutional protections which those in many other countries enjoy.

CHAPTER THREE

PARLIAMENT:
THE HOUSE OF COMMONS

This House is sovereign.

(John Major in the constitution debate;
Hansard, col. 1065, 20 February 1997)

The sovereignty of parliament is in theory the rock on which our constitution and our freedoms rest. It is the first mantra to be recited by those who are resistant to change. But how important, for all its much vaunted aura as the representative assembly of our people, is parliament? What checks and balances does it really exercise over government? How effectively does it do its work? Its role, and the extent to which it is actually controlled by the government of the day, is pivotal to any analysis of where power in our country lies. The power, or sovereignty, of parliament is said to be supreme. This is an elegant way of saying that it is total. But total as it may theoretically be, which is alarming enough in itself, this is not the whole enormity. For in normal times it is the power of the executive which is total, because the executive controls and is supported by the heavily corralled block vote of the majority party in parliament. This means that the government is almost invariably able to achieve its aims.

Nor is this likely to change in practice. Peter Mandelson, one of the prime architects of the Labour success at the 1997 election, has put it bluntly: 'Labour members of parliament have been elected in order to carry out the manifesto for which we have received an overwhelming mandate from the public.' In other words, power is centralised in the hands of the government and the duty of its supporters in parliament is to show the discipline and unthinking obedience of the infantrymen – the British Tommys of democracy.

Only when majorities are thin or uncertain is there any doubt about the effective dictatorship of the government in power. We may then see the oddity of a small number of dissident government supporters, or a small party on whom government depends, carrying more clout or ransom potential than the ranks of the opposition put together. This is, of course, because the opposition can be counted on to oppose almost everything proposed by the government, and so the votes of the dissident few can mean the difference between victory and defeat. We saw this, for example, in 1975 to 1979 and again in the dying years of the recent Conservative government when the Tory party's own rebels and the Ulster Unionists increasingly flexed their muscles. But it is comparatively rare, and government can normally bulldoze their proposals through. It is effectively all-powerful, and hence the aptness of Lord Hailsham's recognition of our 'elective dictatorship'.

In practice, too, the supremacy of parliament means that of one House only: the House of Commons. The unelected House of Lords is fearful to exercise some of its powers because of its doubts about the legitimacy of opposing the will of the elected House of Commons. As a result, when it really matters we are virtually a unicameral country: that is to say we are for the most part dependent for our rights and liberties on a single house of legislators. So how the House of Commons works, and how it is elected, matters vitally. It should be the starting point of constitutional reform, for it affects all other changes. Lord Cranborne, the last leader of the House of Lords, has said that reform of that House could sensibly be considered only alongside changes to the House of Commons. He is surely right in principle. Not only does the way in which one House works affect the other. But the House of Commons is the dominant chamber, and its dominance over the second chamber is far more powerful than in many other constitutions, such as those of the United States and Australia. In those countries the second chambers are wholly elected, but on different voting principles from the first chambers. This reflects the need to secure representation from the various regions or states. As a result, the second chambers have real power and influence. This is not so with our current, wholly unelected and largely hereditary House of Lords.

Concerns about the independence and effectiveness of the House of Commons matter greatly to all of us. So does its reputation, which is crucially and sadly very low at present. It is not healthy that it should be largely a rubber-stamp on government decisions. Nor is it satisfactory that legislation should often be ill-digested and badly thought out. It insults the people that question time on the nation's affairs is often conducted as a schoolboys' tiff. It should be both robust and searching, and certainly not sanitised, but conducted in a way which recognises that the government is accounting to the nation on important issues. MPs should not, as the respondents to a Joseph Rowntree Reform Trust/MORI poll emphatically agreed, receive fees for lobbying on behalf of clients at Westminster. It goes without question, as Lord Nolan has said, that questions in parliament should not be asked for money. The independence of the member of parliament is a crucial attribute. Yet it has dwindled. The vote of salaried ministers, often called the 'payroll' vote (and about 100-strong), is large and wholly tame. Those aspiring to be ministers have to toe the line as the whips go about their work of warning against dissent, and dangling the bait of government office at some future time. It also matters if there is no real job for back-benchers, the members who hold no office. The select committees were a notable development, but have some way to go to be really effective. They should increasingly be strengthened, with a salaried chairman in recognition of his workload. The committees should have the power to call not just ministers but also senior civil servants to account. A public appearance before such a committee is already a demanding occasion, and all of them should become even more knowledgeable and expert. This would help to give many back-benchers a proper role and so make good use of real talent. Contrast the impotent position of many of our back-benchers with the way in which US senators of ability are able to gain real stature in the community for their work in Congress, even if they never hold a government post. The new government has a large number of MPs who will inevitably not hold ministerial office, at any rate in the near future.

So the autonomy, influence and integrity of the member of parliament should wherever possible be raised. The wishes of cabinet should not be taken as being simply final and immune from reasoned discussion. This turns debates into a charade, and renders committee work less effective than it should be. MPs should have more individual responsibility, and they should be better paid. This would also lessen the temptation to seek other employment solely for the money. Surely, too, we have simply too many members of parliament, and could profitably reduce their numbers from the current total of 659. After all, there are only 438 congressmen in the United States House of Representatives. They represent a population four and a half times as large as the UK. Fewer MPs could be better served and more efficient and effective than the heaving herded mass seen in the voting lobbies and crammed into the confines of the Palace of Westminster. The standing of MPs might also be increased if they had greater responsibility and there were fewer of them. The House of Commons does not govern, but, as Gladstone said, its role is to hold government accountable and to shape our laws. This should be a key role for back-benchers to play, and is vital if parliament is to be attuned to the needs and views of the people. MPs can inject the views of their local constituents directly into our law-making process. They should not simply be treated as foot-soldiers to be marched in whichever direction the government wills. Indeed, as parliament passes ever more laws, affecting ever more areas of life, an independent input from experienced MPs is needed more than ever.

Yet members of parliament themselves are not quick to promote change. In February 1997 there was a full-scale debate on the constitution. The chamber did not stay full for long after the adversarial combat between John Major and Tony Blair, who both focused primarily on the issue of devolution for Scotland and Wales. But once the House thinned out there were some notably thoughtful contributions. Tim Eggar suggested that there were too many MPs and that most comparable legislatures had about 400 members, rather than the 650 in the House of Commons. He also stressed the importance of raising the status of senior members and in particular chairmen of committees. He questioned the need for so many junior members of the government, comprising the payroll vote. Tim Rathbone argued that we should have a mechanism for confirming that our own domestic legislation is consistent with the European Convention on Human Rights. He stressed the need to devise an electoral system which ensured proper representation of minorities.

But, for the most part, the speakers in the debate gave little hint that the procedures and work of the House of Commons could be improved. This tends to reflect the insulation of members of parliament from outside views. There is something of a club atmosphere, wrapping members in a pall of complacent self-importance, which they all too glibly justify by their consciousness of the dignity and privileges of parliament. To the external observer, it was hard to understand the fuss about the simple and sensible Nolan Committee recommendation that income should be declared by members.

After all, it would now be unthinkable for the salaries of judges, ministers, senior civil servants or even directors of public companies not to be disclosed. Yet many members of parliament who would describe their work as the highest form of public service were surprisingly bashful about open disclosure of their earnings. Even the then government actually refused to back the principle, which was recommended by the very committee it had set up to advise. A resolution to give effect to this was only carried in the face of government opposition.

Nor did that government subsequently show any urgency about reassuring the public of the financial integrity of its members. A committee was set up under Sir Gordon Downey, the parliamentary commissioner for standards, who is charged with keeping the register of MPs' interests, investigating complaints about failure to declare interests, about the conduct of MPs, and whether they are complying with any code of conduct which the House of Commons adopts. This committee had a mammoth task. It had not completed its work at the time when the 1997 general election was announced. But the government brought in an early prorogation of parliament, well in advance of its formal dissolution. This had the effect that the Downey Report could not be presented to parliament and so, according to its procedures, could apparently not be made available to the public. It was far from clear why the prorogation of parliament could not be delayed to allow the report to be finalised. Those candidates for parliament who were potentially affected by the report became publicly known. Two stood down, and others went into the election with uncertainty hanging over them. But there was a worse dilemma for the voters. They were asked to re-elect candidates without knowing one way or the other whether they had breached proper standards of integrity. This saga gave the impression that the then government was over-concerned to guard the privileges of its MPs without regard for the public whom those privileges are ultimately intended to serve. All professions, whether barristers, journalists or doctors, tend to see issues from their own vantage point. But equally all fall into danger if they do not stand back from their own traditions and ensure that these evolve in a way which meets expectations. It is unacceptable for parliament to legislate in all areas of life it sees fit, if at the same time it cocoons its own practices with such indifference to public opinion.

One crucial role of parliament is enacting a high quality of legislation. We have an immense amount of legislation. In 1900 the statute book ran to 281 pages. In 1994 it filled 2,361 pages; the Finance Act alone came to a total of 463 pages. The failure to 'think through' proposed changes has sometimes led to some notably inept legislation.

In recent years, the 1986 pensions legislation, which encouraged opting out of state pensions, and the poll tax spring to mind. Smaller illustrations of muddle, omission and lack of clarity are legion. Legislation is often hastily conceived, badly drafted through imprecise instructions or pressure of time, and ineffectively debated. As Professor Anthony King of Essex University has pointed out, a recent Education Bill was amended 278 times in the Commons committee stage, 78 more on report, 258 times during the Lords committee stage, 296 more on the next report, and 71 times at third reading: a total of 981 amendments.

In most cases government MPs are expected to support the first and each subsequent version of a bill equally blindly. Typically only amendments introduced by the government have any chance of being accepted. As the fiction that the government knows best, or can get it right first time, is obviously absurd, so is the failure of back-bench MPs to exercise any significant independent influence on the framing and deliberation of legislation.

There is wide recognition that the processes of legislation need to be improved. John Major, in a speech on the constitution in 1996, voiced the concern about the speed with which detailed legislative proposals are prepared and put through both Houses. He suggested a more structured planning of the programme of law-making with more time for consultation, so that each year the government programme would lay out not only plans for legislation covering the year ahead, but provisional plans for what would follow a year later. This would enable more widespread consultation. Select committees could take evidence and report on legislative proposals, and so have a more positive and creative role in the policy process and in the quality of legislation. There is some guidance at hand as to how such a process should be worked. In 1994 the Deregulation and Contracting-Out Act was passed, with the aim of enabling the government to rid business and individuals of regulations which impeded freedom of trade and which were no longer necessary to protect the public. A broad power to enable acts of parliament to be dispensed with by secondary legislation was novel. So a careful procedure was devised to ensure proper opportunity for scrutiny. This procedure is built into the act itself. How does it work?

When the government is considering introducing a deregulation proposal, it first has to consult widely with interested parties. In the light of this initial consultation it can put forward a proposal to both Houses of parliament for their consideration. Each House has a committee to look at the proposal in some detail. The government sends the committees a memorandum which sets out the reasons for the proposal and what its effect would be, and summarises the points raised in the consultation process. The committees, too, can seek out evidence and must have regard to any material which is volunteered to them. In the light of this, each committee, which works separately from the other but with sensible liaison, reports on whether the proposal is sound and suggests possible improvements to take account of the views which have come out in consultation. After this the government frames its final proposals. Key to the process is wide-ranging consultation before any proposal is made at all, and then the opportunity to think again in the light of what the committees of the two Houses say.

This new but effective system could serve as a model of consultation procedure for primary legislation itself. If secondary legislation warrants such thoroughness, surely primary legislation calls for it even more? In 1996 Mr Roger Freeman, then the cabinet minister responsible for deregulation, agreed with the House of Lords committee that the deregulation procedure might well provide valuable learning experience for the better consideration of legislation. Perhaps the Pensions Act, the Child Support Act, the Criminal Justice Act 1991 with its 'unit fines' and its limitations on the extent to which account could be taken of the previous convictions of offenders, and above all the poll tax legislation might have benefited from more structured processes. Too much legislation is ill thought out, too simplistic in its aims, and lacks the input of those who are deeply knowledgeable on complex topics. Nor, in the hurry in which it is produced, does it isolate items of constitutional significance. There are so many reasons for proper consultation. Good debate throws up difficulties, anomalies, and unconsidered situations. Above all it gives those who may be affected the chance to contribute their views and experience. There is real scope here for change.

The standards of law-making are not just a recondite topic of particular interest to lawyers and academics. They impact on us all, and we are all affected by their quality. As Sir Henry Brooke, the former chairman of the Law Commission, said in the Law Commission's 28th Annual Report:

> Much of our law is riddled with faults and flaws . . . and it is often only the imagination and ingenuity of our judges which conceals with judicial sticking-plaster the depth of the fault-lines. The position is now serious. It is not of course cataclysmic. But history shows that a nation which neglects the ordinary

care of its laws is neglecting something which is very important to its national well-being.

To improve the processes of legislation would both give a real measure of practical constitutional reform and enhance the working and authority of parliament.

Interestingly, proposals for a Scottish parliament suggest that members should have the power to initiate as well as comment on legislation. They also anticipate that there should be much closer relationships with groups in society such as organisations of employers and workers and professional bodies to help them both shape and monitor legislation. It would obviously help this process and avoid unnecessary waste at the end of a parliamentary session if legislation could be carried forward from one session to another.

There would be wide agreement that we could do much to improve the way we legislate. It is highly welcome that the government appears to have adopted the proposal to publish in draft for public consultation bills which are to be introduced in future sessions. The establishment of a select committee to consider how practice and procedure should be modernised is most timely. But there is no such agreement about the most fundamental issue of all, the way in which we should elect MPs. Yet this is the single key constitutional issue which needs resolving to give full legitimacy to our democratic government. The ability of a strong government to railroad its proposals through with the backing of a large majority representing less than half the electorate strikes at the heart of representative government. The two main political parties have for long been wedded to the 'first-past-the-post' system which has meant that they have alternated in office for more than seventy years. But there are signs that this consensus may at last break apart. The Labour party has indicated its support for a referendum on proportional representation, and the Liberal Democrats, with slightly under fifty MPs, positively favour change.

Our present system, used to it as we all are, is not historically embedded in the stone of centuries. Until 1885 there were some multi-member constituencies, with a voting system which could mean the election of members from different parties. Gladstone, for example, sat for several multi-member seats. In 1874 he came in second at Greenwich, trailing an MP from the opposing party. But he was nonetheless elected because the constituency was entitled to two members. Over his long parliamentary career Gladstone sat as an MP for five constituencies, and, while undoubtedly a great statesman, he does appear to have regarded the constituencies simply as a route into parliament, and was himself often absent from his constituency. During one prolonged three-year absence from Greenwich, Queen Victoria teasingly offered him a local grace-and-favour house 'in order to ease the discharge of his constituency duties'. The offer was firmly declined.

The change to what became our present first-past-the-post system was initially far from popular. By 1918 many politicians favoured more radical change to proportional representation. In 1918 the House of Commons voted to change to one such system called the alternative vote. But the House of Lords favoured a different system called the single transferable vote. The fairly last-minute but in the event enduring compromise was to stick to the existing system for the 1918 election. From then on, with Labour overtaking the Liberals as one of the two dominant parties, the argument for proportional representation seems to have lost political potency. But this episode reminds us of two things: our present voting system has not always been with us, and people, even if they favour change, will not easily agree what is the best form of replacement.

There should surely now be constructive and cross-party debate on whether change to some system of proportional representation would be worth while. In the four elections before 1997 the Conservatives won overall majorities, in all but the last of them large majorities, with shares of the vote between 42 per cent and 45 per cent. Or, to put it another way, nearly 60 per cent of the voters did not get the government of their choice. The same is true of the last election, yet Labour won a remarkable landslide. Defenders of this outcome would argue that at least we get strong government. But this does not make the system of choice fair. All the more is this so where government is effectively all-powerful. Any democratic electoral process should surely pass first and foremost the test of fairness. Proportional representation comes in many varieties, and devising formulas is great sport for its adherents. This makes it easy for its opponents to mock and play a spoiling game. But it has the priceless advantage that it seeks to be fair and give more of our citizens more of a say in the way they are governed.

The debate should not founder because of disagreement as to which form of electoral system is the best one. None is perfect. But interesting alternatives to our first-past-the-post system have been successfully implemented in other countries.

There is the alternative vote. Under this system members continue to be chosen in their individual constituencies. But voters do not simply pick their one preferred candidate. They list all the candidates in order of preference. If the first count does not produce a candidate with an overall majority, the candidate with the fewest first preferences then exits the contest. His votes go to the candidates whom his voters had marked as second choice, and the process goes on until someone wins an overall majority. The system may sound complex, but it is used effectively to choose the House of Representatives, or lower house, in Australia. A variant of this system is also used in French national elections. While constitutional scholars would say this was not proportional representation, it means at least that a greater number of votes count than under our present first-past-the-post system.

A second approach is that described as the single transferable vote. Here constituencies have more than one member. Voters again choose their preferred candidate and there is a similar elimination procedure as that under the alternative vote system. The difference is that, once a candidate has gained enough votes to be elected, a second member is chosen with the surplus votes of the first candidate redistributed according to second preferences. This is the system which governs elections in Ireland and some elections in the states of Australia.

The third variant is what is called an additional member system. One tranche of seats is distributed to the candidates who come first in individual constituencies. This is calculated on a straight majority vote. But then the share which each party has won of the total national vote is assessed. Seats are allocated to parties from their own national lists of candidates so that their overall total number of seats in the legislature, including those which they have gained in constituencies, is in proportion to their share of the national vote. In Germany this system operates with half the seats being allocated to the national list. But there can also be a protection against fringe parties with minimal support gaining seats, and so having the opportunity to influence the balance of power. For example in Germany no party wins any seats from the list unless it either scores 5 per cent of the national vote or wins at least three individual constituency seats. The additional member system is also used in Belgium, Denmark and Sweden.

This additional member system has the considerable attraction of being the fairest in principle. It means that each party effectively gets as many seats as its share of the national vote warrants. But it also provides representation for the individual constituencies. The drawback is that members of the legislature will fall into two categories: those who have won an individual constituency, and those who have simply been nominated from a party list. Nomination from the party list is likely to produce more members who are slavishly and blindly loyal to the party line because they are even more dependent on patronage. Those members chosen from the national list will not have any constituency or grass-root links.

Yet, as parliamentarians here agree, this is one of the most valuable assets of individual members. Their role as welfare officer for the constituents, with the need to be part of constituency life, means that they are particularly close to the thinking of their supporters and fairly knowledgeable about the overall mood in the constituency. Writing, complaining and talking to their MP is one way in which citizens can get closer to government. Most MPs take this duty very seriously. Any change to the voting system should seek to preserve this important point of local contact.

So the fairness of the additional member system has to be balanced against the extent to which it could remove some members from contact with the electorate. One of the other methods might better meet the United Kingdom tradition, with the single transferable vote having the attraction that constituencies with more than one member of different political persuasions would give more constituents a feeling that they were directly represented. This is my own tentative personal preference. But the experience of other mature and effective democracies indicates that each of the systems can be workable.

Defenders of the existing position tend to point to the dangers of the unknown. They remind us that Italy, with its system of proportional representation, has had well over fifty governments since the war, or that in Germany the third party carries disproportionate influence in coalitions. But systems which have worked respectively in Australia, Ireland and Germany can surely each command respect. Can any of these countries be said to have been conspicuously worse governed than the United Kingdom over the past fifty years? Can there be said to have been less national harmony? Less efficient economics? Less fairness in addressing social issues?

Nor are the familiar arguments favouring strong government over-impressive. There are objections in principle to strong government. We would not accept dictatorship to secure strong government. Why should we be prepared to achieve it by perpetuating a distortion of democracy? It can also be cogently urged that in practice there are many times when a government should seek as wide a consensus as possible. There is now broad agreement in this country on the fundamentals of sound economic management. But on the prioritisation and management of microeconomic and social issues, and on constitutional change, important debate is in train. To this debate the closest involvement of representatives of the people and the greatest achievable consensus is important.

But what is even more fundamental is that the system of election, which is currently the only power the people have over government, should be fair. For lack of fairness will slowly eat away at the fabric of democracy. Some of our people are in effect permanently disenfranchised, excluded from any meaningful part in democracy, and minorities may so easily be overlooked or short-changed. This is contrary to the warning of Thomas Jefferson, expressed in his first Inaugural Address: 'This sacred principle, that though the will of the majority is in all cases to prevail, that will, to be rightful, must be reasonable; that the minority possess their equal rights, which equal laws must protect, and to violate which would be oppression.' Equal rights must surely include equal representation in shaping the laws of our country. Or at very least our people need the chance to say in a referendum whether they, too, see it that way. They need to have the opportunity to decide whether they are content to support a voting system where a minority of the voters elects a government for five years and allows that government to do what it will in between with many of our people hopelessly under-represented in the legislature. The very foundation of our democracy is currently fragile and that carries marked dangers for society.

CHAPTER FOUR

PARLIAMENT: THE HOUSE OF LORDS

The weakness of the Lords is that it is able to do too little and not that it is able to do too much.

(Lord Hailsham of St Marylebone,
The Dilemma of Democracy, *1978)*

There is a temptation for views about the House of Lords to take their tone from its physical setting. The graceful stonework, created to the architectural design of Sir Charles Barry and burnished with the splendidly vivid decorative arts of Pugin, is impressively majestic. There is an air of continuity, of longevity and of a weighty, deliberative assembly. It all seems more dignified and sumptuous than the workaday surroundings of the immediately adjoining House of Commons. New peers waiting at the doors of the chamber to be summoned can almost physically feel the weight of history and an aura of long-standing importance. But in truth how much of a role has history now left to what was once generally called the 'Upper House'?

The modern subordinate role of the House of Lords is much the same age as the building, constructed as part of the renaissance of the Houses of parliament after the dramatic fire of 1834. For several hundred years before the great Reform Act 1832, power had gradually been lost to the Commons. Even in the eighteenth century the Whig aristocrats who dominated politics tended to do so because of their

69

control of family and placemen in the House of Commons. The greatest statesmen of that century all led the nation from the House of Commons: Walpole and the two William Pitts. But it was the battle over parliamentary reform in the first half of the nineteenth century which established the clear and emphatic dominance of the House of Commons as the source of power.

The general election of 1831 was fought on the issue of parliamentary reform, the extension of the franchise for election to the House of Commons, and the reformers won a famous victory. A Reform Bill duly passed the House of Commons, but was voted down by the Lords in effective defiance of the election result. The Lords was massively Tory and had a strong vested interest in the continuance of the old system. The Commons tried again, and once again the Lords thwarted it. It did not lack chutzpah. It was then that Lord Grey, the prime minister, demanded the creation of at least fifty peers. When King William IV refused to make the appointments, Grey resigned. Undeterred, the king asked the Duke of Wellington to try to form a Tory government. But Wellington failed, largely because he could not find support in the Commons. Grey confronted the king again, and was reappointed, this time with the backing of the promise of the creation of enough peers to enable the bill to pass.

This finally brought the then wholly hereditary House of Lords to heel. It saw no attraction in allowing any dilution of its membership. Meanwhile the bill over which there had been such a constitutional rumpus made only a modest extension to the vote, adding 300,000 to an existing franchise of 350,000 out of a population of sixteen million people. But at least it opened the way to the slow but steady series of further extensions until full adult suffrage was achieved almost a hundred years later.

The influence of the peerage did not immediately die with this defeat. For a long time to come the aristocracy was very well represented by family connections in the House of

Commons. They had, as all readers of the novels of Trollope know, a real but gradually diminishing power to influence the election of members to seats. They also had a part in cabinet wholly disproportionate to the power of their legislative chamber. As late as the 1900s, Lord Salisbury's cabinet contained twelve peers out of twenty members. But, for all this lingering influence, and some later flare-ups, the importance of the House of Lords was much diminished. From 1832 onwards it was undoubtedly the subordinate chamber. But it still had the power to reject bills and thwart the will of the Commons.

In 1867, on the eve of the second Reform Act, which raised the number of voters to 2,500,000, Walter Bagehot wrote in *The English Constitution* that the House had become 'a second-rate force'. Bagehot's assessment was part reality, part prophecy, and increasingly proved accurate, but not without bumps on the way. Ireland, the cause of so many fault-lines across British politics, led to a reassertion of power by the House of Lords some sixty years after its defeat over the first Reform Act. Gladstone, who had come out for home rule for Ireland in 1886, had the opportunity after his last election victory of introducing an Irish Home Rule Bill in 1893. With the combined vote of his Liberal party and the Irish, it passed through the House of Commons. But the House of Lords refused to accept that the will of the people favoured the measure. Lord Salisbury summed up for the opposition: 'We hope that the people will support us to abide by the Union of the United Kingdom which we believe was decreed by nature and to which laws and treaties have only given a written sanction and record.' This appeal to apparently immutable law no doubt had the advantage for its advocates that the solid vote of the Irish MPs for home rule could be conveniently ignored. The Union had been imposed almost a century earlier, following violence and rebellions in Ireland, as a means of controlling what was seen as a barbarous and unruly country. Much the same distaste and a wish to control the Irish underlay the rejection of Gladstone's bill. But rejected it was, by 419 votes to 41. Gladstone had no opportunity to try again. No one can predict the way in which history would have been different if home rule had been granted. Yet many feel that much of the unfinished violence and conflict of this century would have been avoided.

One constant and enduring characteristic of the Lords since the Reform Act has been the existence of a perpetual and substantial Conservative majority. This inevitably meant that historically there was less, if any, challenge to the legislation of Conservative governments than to those of other complexions. So it is no surprise that, strengthened in resolve by its victory over home rule, the Lords' muscles were flexed again in conflict with the Liberal government elected in 1906. That this government had just won a decisive election victory failed to deter the peers. They dismembered the Education Bill introduced the same year. They went on successfully to oppose one of the two most sweeping programmes for social reform of this century, destroying among others both a licensing bill and another education bill. The crunch came with Lloyd George's budget in April 1909. Super taxes and land taxes were at the heart of the dispute. In resisting these, the Conservative majority in the Lords tilted at what the Commons considered to be its sole constitutional right to shape and legislate for finance bills. The budget was thrown out by 350 votes to 75.

An election inevitably followed, which the Liberals won inconclusively. They needed to rely in the House of Commons on the votes of the Irish nationalists. Attempts to broker a compromise failed. There was a second general election later in 1910 with almost the same result as the earlier one. Asquith, the prime minister, secured, as Grey had done almost eighty years before him, a promise from the king, George V, to create a vast number of peers to enable him to carry through a bill to reform the House of Lords. Even so, a number of opposition peers aptly known as 'die-hards' would have rejected these reforms. But the threat of nearly 500 new peers was seen by the majority as mixing too much vinegar with the wine and the bill scraped home. Interestingly the preamble to the bill shows that this was only to be the first measure of reform: 'And whereas it is intended to substitute for the House of Lords as it at present exists a Second Chamber constituted on a popular instead of hereditary basis, but such substitution cannot immediately be brought into operation.' The act also provided that if any other bill, except one extending the life of a parliament, were passed in the House of Commons in three sessions, and two years had passed between the first second reading in the Commons and its final passing, the Commons could insist that the bill become law, even if it had been rejected by the Lords. In addition, the House of Lords lost any power to reject 'money' bills at all and now by convention does not even debate the annual Finance Bill.

A committee chaired by Lord Rosebery, the former prime minister, had recommended in 1908 that the balance of parliament required a strong and efficient second chamber, to be achieved by reform and reconstitution of the Lords, and that as a preliminary to reform it should be accepted that the possession of a peerage should no longer of itself entail the right to sit and vote. No action was taken on this report. Nor did a government proposal in 1922 proposing a House of Lords of 350 members, with some elected, some chosen by hereditary peers, and some nominated by the Crown, find any favour. In 1934 Lord Salisbury's Parliament (Reform) Bill was dropped. The argument surfaced from time to time but lacked urgency. Why?

Between 1914 and 1945 two world wars, and governments which were mostly coalition or Conservative with only two brief periods of Labour, meant that there was no real potential for conflict between the two houses. But in 1945 the Labour government, with its own dramatic programme of economic and social reform, came to power. The Conservatives, under the realistic and pragmatic leadership of Lord Salisbury, for some time avoided conflict. He shaped the doctrine that the opposition would not reject bills which formed part of the government's manifesto commitments and so were part of a successful general election platform. Nonetheless the proposal to nationalise iron and steel raised the prospect of head-on collision. So the government introduced a new Parliament Bill which was at first rejected by the Lords but eventually passed automatically into law, pursuant to the terms of the Parliament Act 1911. The 1949 act in its turn cut short the period for which the Lords could delay legislation by reducing the number of sessions in which the bill must be passed by the Commons from three to two, and by reducing the period between first and second reading and final passing in the Commons from two years to one. This meant that the Lords could not successfully defy the government for too long, and particularly could not block legislation in the second half of a parliament in the hope of gaining time until an election.

These two Parliament Acts had effectively formalised what Bagehot had described almost a century before as the power of the House of Lords temporarily to reject measures. Ironically since 1949 there has been only one occasion on which the Parliament Act has been used. This was in 1991. Mrs Thatcher's government had introduced a War Crimes Bill. A House of Lords dominated by Conservative peers, who were so often among her staunchest admirers, rejected the bill on 4 June 1990. The Parliament Act was invoked, and the bill received royal assent on 9 May 1991, shortly after the Lords had rejected it for the second time. So far incidentally there have been no successful prosecutions under the act.

This brief history shows not only how the Lords came to have its present limited role. It also demonstrates that on each of the great issues on which it chose to fight – reform, home rule for Ireland, and the people's budget – the Lords was sadly out of touch with the great issues of the times. Even more fundamentally, it demonstrates the impossibility that an unelected House of Lords could sensibly claim that greater powers should be granted to the second chamber. The price for greater power would have to be some form of representatively elected chamber. A trade-off between greater powers and elections would be worth serious consideration. Yet it is not at present in the realm of practical politics. It is on no political agenda. Change in the composition of the House of Lords is squarely on the government's agenda. But no political party has as any part of its agenda proposals to change the functions of the House of Lords. Nor is there any popular pressure for the grant of increased powers. What this means is that we have a second chamber which is very limited in its power and influence. It is also, because it is hopelessly undemocratic in composition, unwilling to use what powers it has robustly.

The United States provides an interesting and striking contrast. The two houses within Congress, the House of Representatives and the Senate, are equal in authority. They are elected under different voting systems which are designed to protect different interests within a federation. Each state elects to the House of Representatives a number of members proportionate to the population of that state. By contrast, each state, whatever its population, is entitled to two senators. This means that the House and the Senate can sometimes fall under different political control but in any event are democratically elected. The president is frequently from a different political party from the one which controls Congress. All this adds another dimension to the checks and balances in a country whose states differ widely in their geography, economy and social influences. This division of powers can sometimes be an obstacle to decisive government. But it is a considerable restraint against an over-powerful government riding rough-shod over interests with which it disagrees.

The Australian constitution divides legislative power between its two Houses of parliament in much the same way. While part of the distinction reflects the federal structures of those two countries, in each the second chamber has significant power over every important legislative issue, including finance bills.

This puts our own position in stark relief. The power in our legislature rests almost entirely in the House of Commons. When we speak grandiosely about the sovereignty of parliament, we are in reality speaking simply of the elected chamber. We are not speaking even remotely of co-equal branches of the legislature. But what is remarkable, and one of the paradoxes of the survival of the House of Lords, is that some of its work is essential and of real quality. This is because of its role as a revising chamber. To improve, and refine, legislation is at the heart of the work of the Lords and makes a major contribution in an area where, as we have seen, the Commons lacks strength and inclination. It occupies much of the time of the Lords: the House often sits until well after ten at night. The work calls for patient, non-histrionic, wide-ranging and thoughtful expertise. These qualities are strikingly present. Interestingly the work is done mostly, although not solely, by life peers.

The pressures of modern government on parliamentary time make its use extremely precious. To get its legislation through, the government divides the workload between the two Houses. Shortly after the Queen's Speech, which is normally in the autumn, some bills are introduced in the Commons and some in the Lords. These bills complete their stages in the respective Houses before Easter, and then go to the other House. When a bill is first introduced in the Lords, it is sometimes uninhibited in proposing significant change. In 1994 there was a strong protest against the proposal in the Police Bill to bring appointments to police authorities under greater Home Office control. The government felt constrained to back down from its initial proposal and allow a good deal more independent local input and autonomy. In the Divorce Bill in 1995 some radical changes were made, under vociferous cross-party pressure, to the proposals in the bill. Not the least of the successes in the Lords was to pave the way for a government concession that pensions should be split between husband and wife on divorce. In the Broadcasting Bill the Lords overturned much of the government's proposal to concede many major sporting events to satellite television.

My impression is that the Lords is in practice less inhibited in proposing amendments to government bills where those bills start in the Lords than when they start in the Commons. By contrast it often seems much more cautious once the Commons has given its approval to the shape of a particular bill. Whatever its formal powers, it largely defers to the wishes of the elected chamber. So in one sense it can all depend on the allocation of the workload whether the Lords makes a real impact on a bill. In logic, and constitutionally, it should not be so, but in practice it is.

One of the most important changes made to legislation in recent years by the Lords was in other legislation which started there: the Police Act 1997. For some years the police had been using powers to trespass on, or interfere with, property, including homes and offices, to obtain information electronically by bugging. The power was used when it was thought by senior police officers to be valuable in the investigation of serious crime. It had been exercised for twenty years under administrative guidelines but without any legal authority and totally contrary to what many people had regarded as the constitutional doctrine that 'an Englishman's home is his castle'. This had been the law since even the autocratic, pre-democratic days of George III. Yet by 1995 across the United Kingdom police and Customs and Excise had carried out these surveillance exercises on no fewer than 2,000 occasions in a single year. They had not been given legal power to do so. The Home Office had authorised it simply under administrative guidelines. But who in the Home Office? It emerged in debate that three successive home secretaries of real stature, Roy Jenkins, James Callaghan and Robert Carr, had apparently not been informed of what was being done in the name of their department. So the government, belatedly and rightly, decided, with full police support, to seek statutory powers for what was being done.

Once they did so concerns were increasingly raised about the way in which the powers were to be authorised. The proposal was that senior police officers should authorise their own forces to carry out the surveillances. This was contrary to the way permission is granted in other civilised countries, where a judicial warrant prior to the surveillance is regarded as fundamental. Why? Because the right to privacy of and in the home is a precious one. The police have an impossible task if they are to be asked to detect crime but also somehow to weigh individual liberties in the balance. Their emphasis is understandably bound to be on the pursuit of crime. Indeed so precious is the need for the protection of a judge in the United States that it is enshrined in the Fourth Amendment of the constitution. The laws of Canada, New Zealand, Australia, France and Germany all have the same effect.

Lord Browne-Wilkinson had previously attempted to alert the Lords to a similar erosion of liberties contained in the Security Services Act 1996. That act gave MI5 a role not only in areas which affect national security, such as espionage, but in the investigation of serious crime. They were to be able to reinforce police activity. The legislation granted MI5 agents, provided that they had the home secretary's approval, the power of searching properties, tapping telephones, intercepting post and bugging anyone they believed to be taking part in serious criminal activities. He described this extension of powers as 'a major constitutional shift' and a threat to individual liberty. But his concerns struck no chord at all in the House, which was massively uninterested, and so the proposal passed into law. When the Police Bill came forward some months later, both government and Labour opposition at first seemed wholly unconcerned about the constitutional issues. But then individual members came in powerfully on the side of civil liberties. The cause united newspapers whose opinions often differ sharply: from *The Times* and the *Daily*

Telegraph to the *Guardian* and *Observer*. The *Daily Mail*, too, was roused, partly by the fear that its offices would be bugged. The Lords now awoke fully to the danger to liberty of the proposal that the police could authorise themselves, and insisted on prior judicial authorisation. The amendments were carried by large majorities and the government in the end grudgingly and complainingly backed down. It did not accept the whole principle of the change, watering it down, but did at least include some independent judicial safeguards. The Lords had struck a blow for civil liberties.

This was a comparatively rare act of resistance by the Lords and shows its residual power when it has the confidence to act. In this case it gained confidence because the peers realised from all the press reports that the public was on their side. Popular opinion gave legitimacy to their cause and made them bold.

But whether a bill begins in the Lords or the Commons, it is the Lords which goes through it clause by clause and line by line to test its meaning, its effectiveness, and to seek to fine down rough edges. With parliamentary draftsmen over-worked, and legislation often not exposed to prior consultation, this is badly needed. The Commons committees, which rarely involve the whole House, tend to argue and vote on political issues along largely party lines. They are less concerned with the quality of the legislation. Often they do not have adequate expertise or research assistance. Nor are all the amendments in the Lords simply matters of drafting. Often issues of real substance can be raised because of the expertise on the particular topic of individual members of the House. Since the various stages of the bill are usually taken on the floor of the House, members can join in to participate on individual issues on which they have expertise. The process sometimes seems to grind slowly but it grinds surely: second reading speeches may indicate important issues of concern, and the committee and report stages can shape the bill. Where views are expressed with strength across party lines, negotiations can lead to an agreed amendment. As Lord Denham, a skilled and popular former government chief whip, has said, the number of times the government is beaten in the division lobbies is far from a full reflection of the extent to which the Lords alters legislation. Revising legislation is an important and not a recondite role. The thrust of legislation, and its efficiency, are vital to the citizen and to the courts, which are so often called upon to adjudicate its effects. The quality of our law affects us all.

Obviously the virtues of this revising role can be overstated. Frequently the amendments made are introduced by government as an afterthought or to improve previous ill-thought-out proposals. Sometimes House of Lords amendments passed against the government are overridden by the Commons. But there is no doubt that in our present, clumsy and haphazard processes of legislation the Lords both picks up the pieces and improves the outcome.

The Lords also polices the grant of powers of delegated legislation to a government. The Delegated Powers and Deregulation Committee looks at all bills to scrutinise where they propose such powers, and advises whether these powers are proper for delegation, whether the framework for their exercise is precise and narrow enough, whether there should be consultation before they are exercised, and what kind of parliamentary scrutiny is necessary. The committee approaches its task as one of constitutional principle and is in no sense party political. The last government had an excellent record of implementing the committee's recommendations. If, as John Major thoughtfully suggested, a new two-year rolling programme of legislation were to be adopted, the role of the House of Lords could be enhanced and its efficiency improved. It could adapt its work so that its committees were able to react to consultation, and suggest improvements, at an early stage. The new government has indicated its commitment to publishing for consultation draft bills which it intends to bring forward in future sessions. Here the Lords can bring real value: experience, a relative lack of partisan bias and an undoubted concern for minorities. Above all it would not be driven simply by the adversarial conflict of the Commons.

So to me this revising, or improving, role is the key function of the House of Lords. The influence of some of its other work is often disappointingly slight. There are select committees on important issues such as the European Community, and science and technology. Their work is detailed, informed and draws on an expert membership. But it attracts little publicity, and it is far from clear what influence it has with government. The same is true of question time. The chamber is full, issues are probed, and as in the Commons the government often stonewalls and gives as little valuable information as possible. In any event the responsible minister is normally not in the Lords and so cannot be called to account directly but only through his deputy. There are general debates every Wednesday, often on an important economic, educational or social topic. The standard of contributions can be high, although the atmosphere is sometimes a touch self-congratulatory. But these debates rarely have much influence and the members all too often seem to be talking to themselves as in an echo chamber.

Nor does the Lords make vigorous use of its other undoubted powers, with the rare exception of the Police Act, mentioned earlier. It almost never relies on the delaying power, even though it has a clear statutory basis, affirmed in both 1911 and 1949. In the last decade or so, the Lords did not seek to delay the controversial proposal to abolish the GLC, or the changes to the rating system brought about under the short-lived and ill-fated community charge or poll tax. The power to ask the government to think again about the wisdom of a legislative proposal may not have wholly withered. But it seems virtually to have done so. Nor is the House more vigorous in exercising its power over secondary legislation. The Lords has currently a self-denying ordinance by which it declines, whatever its own views, to vote down government proposals which require an affirmative resolution to come into force. This voluntary abdication of its power, and indeed its duty, means that the Lords does not even try to act as a delaying chamber to hold up what it thinks of as bad secondary legislation. This legislation consists of the mass of regulations which ministers have power to make. Many of these have to be approved by parliament but, if the Lords declines ever to strike any of them down, the process of approval then becomes no more than a charade.

The reluctance of the Lords to challenge the Commons at all was recently demonstrated in the Asylum and Immigration Bill. In early 1996, Peter Lilley, the secretary of state for social security, driven by concern about the increasing claims for benefit by asylum-seekers while waiting for their applications to be decided, introduced a regulation providing that no one should be eligible for benefit unless they made their claim for asylum immediately on arriving in this country. Some months later, the Court of Appeal declared that these regulations were outside the scope of his powers.

The Asylum and Immigration Bill happened to be going through parliament at the same time. So the home secretary brought in a speedy amendment to achieve the same effect as the proposed regulation which the court had condemned. The Lords accepted this amendment in general terms but also provided that people should have at least up to three days after arrival to make their claim. There was a strong feeling that, on their arrival, asylum-seekers could not always know their rights or might simply be frightened to exercise them. While the statistics show that a high percentage of claims for asylum was rejected, they also demonstrated that the great majority of successful claims were made by those who had only applied for asylum after they had been in the country some time, and not at the port of entry. So there was a solidly based fear that genuine claims might be arbitrarily excluded unless applicants were given time after arrival to make their claim. This amendment was passed by the Lords. But it was overturned in the Commons. When the bill came back to the Lords, there was an attempt to put forward a compromise amendment which allowed people to lodge their claim within three days of arrival provided that they could give firm proof of the date of arrival. A major issue was whether the Lords should defer to the view of the Commons. Lord Simon of Glaisdale, a former law lord and constitutional expert, said that if the Lords 'were to accept that once the [Commons] has expressed a view that is an end of the matter, it would be an abrogation of your Lordships' role in the constitution'. But the Lords declined the opportunity to pursue the view it had previously backed and tamely gave way. It accepted that asylum-seekers might have to live in destitution. This saga demonstrates an ever-present fear which underlies the Lords' work that it must bend over backwards not to come into conflict with the Commons. It is all too conscious of its lack of democratic legitimacy. This often leads it to shy away from exercising its clear constitutional rights which have been buttressed by successive Parliament Acts.

Nor does the Lords have a particular strength in defending what may be thought of as traditional basic liberties. Take the right to silence. For centuries this prevented judge or prosecution from commenting to the jury on the decision of a defendant not to answer questions put to him by the police. The Royal Commission on Criminal Justice, chaired by Viscount Runciman, reported in 1993 that this remained a valuable safeguard for an individual defendant. But the government nonetheless proposed to change the law. The change passed the Commons, and amendments to restore the long-standing existing position failed in the Lords. The argument was that the change would help to catch criminals, or 'malefactors' as one member described them. A good deal of reliance was placed on the position in Northern Ireland, which was said not to have caused any injustice. Later, although not at the time of the debate in the House, Lord Lowry, the former chief justice of Northern Ireland, expressed his doubts as to the wisdom of the change. He saw it as 'embodying contradictions: "You do not have to say anything . . . but if you don't say anything you may be prejudiced at your trial".' It was right to change the law to allow comment at trial if the defendant, when advised by lawyers, did not answer the case against him. But this much more extreme step entitled the police to interrogate him on arrest, or in the cells, and without the benefit of advice from lawyers or relatives or friends. The *Economist* commented that this change 'arguably marks a low-water mark for British civil liberties'.

As the proposer of the unsuccessful amendments, I perhaps not surprisingly agree. But for present purposes the wisdom or otherwise of the change is not the point. What matters is that the Lords was apparently unperturbed by the fact that it was sweeping aside an ancient liberty which had so recently been upheld by a powerful Royal Commission.

But just as disturbing, or perhaps even more so, is the change to our constitution made by a late amendment to the Defamation Bill 1996. The Bill of Rights 1689 has long been regarded as a fundamental part of our constitution. It was part of the settlement which followed the dramatic dismissal from the throne of James II. It aimed to entrench the right to parliamentary government. To this end Article 9 protected the freedom of MPs to speak their minds in the House of Commons, by preventing the courts from questioning all proceedings in parliament. But recently this worked to the disadvantage of Neil Hamilton, a Conservative MP. He had sued the *Guardian* newspaper, which had accused him of accepting cash for tabling parliamentary questions. His action had been unable to continue because it involved exploring or relying on what was said in parliament. Meanwhile a bill to improve access to the courts in defamation cases had commenced its passage through the Lords. At a late stage, Lord Hoffmann, a law lord who had played a part in the promotion of the bill, introduced an amendment to allow a member of parliament to waive the privilege under the Bill of Rights in court actions should he wish to do so. The Lords, after a spirited but comparatively short debate, accepted the amendment. The Commons duly followed in its wake a few weeks later.

This sad saga is of real concern. Those who set their faces against any significant constitutional reform tend to refer to our great constitutional documents, from Magna Carta to the Bill of Rights, as the foundation of our liberties. But this episode showed that a right which had been hard won, and existed unchallenged for 300 years, could be changed at a stroke during the passage of a minor law reform bill. The privilege was a privilege of parliament as a whole, affecting the individual members only in the interests of the good government of the nation. The new amendment allowed the individual member to regard it as his own privilege, to give him the choice to decide to sue where he wished to do so or, in other situations, to rely on the privilege if convenient. There was understandable sympathy at the time for Mr Hamilton, whose attempt to clear his name had apparently been blocked, although this sympathy drained instantly away when he dropped his action at the door of the court.

The wider constitutional issues of this change in the law are alarming. The Lords had every freedom to assert its independent judgement. The government, through the lord chancellor, professed itself to be 'neutral' about the change, although it subsequently claimed it had initiated it. Because the bill had started in the Lords, it was free to shape it without having at that stage to take into account the view of the Commons. But without more ado, and without giving itself the chance to think through the issues of real principle, the Lords voted to change the Bill of Rights. This particular change may not of itself do much harm. But it graphically indicates that none of our constitutional liberties is so firmly embedded as to be immune to the whims of instant politics.

If, by contrast, we had a constitutional commission in this country, it could have raised the red flag.

So, in summary, the powers of the House of Lords are now modest in our largely single-chamber, or unicameral, democracy. The Lords is far from robust in exercising the powers it undoubtedly has. The use of the delaying power is minimal. It currently does not vote against the government on secondary legislation. Nor in fulfilling its functions does it see itself especially as guardian of our liberties. But one aspect of its functions is invaluable, as a revising chamber shaping and improving the legislation which affects all our lives. What, if any, change in the composition of the House is called for?

The single great change in the composition of the Lords in centuries was made possible by the Life Peerage Act 1958. It was almost a hundred years earlier that the Lords itself had rejected the proposal of Lord Palmerston's first government to create life peers. But the much later proposal of Harold Macmillan was widely welcomed, and has made a decisive impact on the mixture of those who do the work of the House. Before then the second chamber had been dying on its feet, but the change gave it a fresh lease of life. There are at present almost 1,300 peers, of whom 770 are hereditary and the rest are life peers. But some in each category attend only sparingly. There are about 400 who attend regularly, split roughly equally between hereditary and life peers. So the influence of the hereditary peers on the House of Lords has been markedly diluted. There is ample scope for the appointment as working peers of people of achievement and knowledge who will bring a special perspective to those areas in which their expertise lies. The Lords as it is at present composed does not lack the talent needed for its role of amending and improving legislation. This is perhaps why the last Conservative government saw no call for change and said, in Lord Melbourne's world-weary phrase, 'Why not let it alone?' It would add for good measure that it is not very expensive, costing at the last tally about £24 million a year.

But this stonewalling has not always been the stance of the Conservative party. As long ago as 1908 a select committee of peers concluded that 'it was undesirable that the possession of a peerage should of itself give the right to sit and vote in the House of Lords'. Between the two world wars there was a steady stream of proposals to amend the composition of the House. Most of them seem to reflect a far-seeing Conservative concern that its members could play a much more effective part in a democratic age if there was a more rational basis than heredity for their appointment. In 1968 proposals to change the composition of the Lords made considerable progress with all major political parties. Change was supported by the front benches of all three parties in both the Lords and the Commons. But it was frustrated in the Commons by a bizarre combination of right and left, led by Enoch Powell and Michael Foot. The essential reason for their opposition was that change would make the Lords more effective. Powell said that it was 'neither desirable nor tolerable that much more than the present degree of check upon the decisions' of the first House should be exercised by the second. In other words there was a vested interest in keeping the Lords weak and a clear acknowledgement that without reform its powers would be unimpressive. No wonder at the end of this saga Lord Carrington said, 'My Lords, it is not your Lordships' fault you are unreformed.'

In 1978 a strong Conservative committee faced up to the problem. Its report included the concern that 'the present House of Lords faces gradual but relentless atrophy; at worst it may be swept away by government impatient of the modest checks it imposes on the passage of legislation'. It proposed direct election of two-thirds of its members by proportional representation, and nomination of the other one-third, as a way of securing a more effective second chamber. But nothing came of this suggestion. At much the same time Lord Hailsham, in *The Dilemma of Democracy*, expressed his belief that the second chamber should be elected, possibly from some very large regional constituencies and from party lists and independents which could include religious leaders. In both these proposals there is a recognition that more effective power could only be given to the Lords if there was a radical change in the composition of the chamber.

There are many other possible recipes for change, plenty of possible permutations. Should there be a number of hereditary peers elected by the whole body of such peers in the way that Irish and Scottish representative peers used to be elected long ago? Some hereditary peers are of great ability and give much of their time to the work of the House and, as sometimes shows, their background is such that no sectional interest owns their souls. Or should there be a more extended list of appointed peers which could include some hereditary peers appointed on ability? The religious element is worth preserving but should it in a more multi-cultural society be less dominated by the Church of England and have greater input from, for example, the Jewish and Muslim faiths? Should the appointments system be more alert to recognise the value people would give to the House if more of them were appointed in their prime, rather than towards the end of their careers? Should there perhaps be membership for terms of years so there could be input from, for example, the serving president of the CBI and the secretary-general of the TUC? Should there be a retiring age? The average age of those currently taking part in the work of the House is nearer to seventy than to sixty. And would representation from the regions, whose interests are so often unheard in the metropolitan hum of our over-centralised society, be a worthwhile counterweight? And if so, should the regional representatives at least be directly elected? Or does legitimacy require that there are far fewer appointed representatives and much more widespread election?

These are but possibilities and there can be a good deal of argument over the right balance. What seems less than convincing is the Labour party proposal to abolish the right of hereditary peers to take part in the work of the House and then, and only then, to decide what is its right composition. To cut off one of the wheels of the car before deciding how to modify its design seems hardly the way to make the vehicle run smoothly. As even a recent Fabian Society pamphlet said: 'The Labour Party's proposals can have no credibility until it publishes a white paper on the final shape and function it envisages' for the second chamber. What is important is a package which gives the House greater efficiency and legitimacy to encourage it to exercise the power it has, rather than shying away from any challenge to the elected chamber. A good package could reduce the numbers, eliminate the hereditary representation, provide safeguards against the appointment of too many party hacks and give the people some say in the membership.

But, whatever method is adopted, there is one issue which has to be grasped in any change which is made. This is the inbuilt and perpetual Conservative majority, based mainly on the great number of hereditary peers. The majority party in the second chamber need not always be of the same political colour as that in the Commons. Indeed if it were always so, unlike the position in the United States and Australia, the second chamber would often be but a rubber-stamp of the Commons. What is unacceptable is for there to be an immutable Conservative majority, whether the Conservatives are in government or opposition. There is no doubt that in its revising role the House has from time to time shown striking independence in the last eighteen years of Conservative government. There have been many rebuffs where the opposition parties, the independent members who sit on the cross-benches and some Conservatives have believed that government proposals needed change. Over 160 amendments were passed against the government between 1979 and 1997, some of them of considerable significance. Nor does this do justice to the changes which are sometimes agreed to by the government in the light of views expressed in debate. But, for all that, in the five years of Labour government from 1974 to 1979, over 350 defeats were inflicted on the government. It is inevitable that an inbuilt Conservative majority will look more critically on the government proposals when their party is in opposition. So the hereditary sway continues to dominate, giving us a legislative chamber still largely ruling by accident of birth.

Any opposition in the Lords will obviously be conscious that it should not obstruct the government too much, that it should not delay the implementation of manifesto commitments, and that it is prudent not to promote too much adversarial conflict with the Commons. I believe strongly that the Lords should not seek to thwart the will of the people, as in 1832 or 1911. Yet a non-Conservative government depends on the acquiescence of the opposition to get its legislation through. Lord Shepherd, who has been both chief whip and leader of the House in Labour governments, has acknowledged the courtesy and co-operation of the then opposition in enabling government business to be done but has nonetheless remarked that the achievements of his government's programme depended upon a 'grace-and-favour' approach from the opposition. This cannot be right, nor can it be good for the authority of the Lords. It would be highly unfortunate if, after being relatively restrained in the exercise of its powers during the Conservative government, the Lords were to become more active, more positive and robust in delaying or altering the legislation of a new Labour government.

So I do not think the present situation can possibly be 'let alone'. The position where all hereditary peers can take part in the work of the Lords has long been thought by so many to be indefensible if the second chamber is to carry any authority. What is the point of a chamber which regards its foundation as so rocky that it shrinks from using its powers? But, over and above that, the composition must be changed to ensure that there is not a permanent, dominant Conservative majority. It is probably good if the Lords is kept at some distance from popular democracy so that it can be reflective in its work. There is no point in the House simply cloning the composition of the Commons. But a greater cross-section of society and a sharp reduction of membership flowing from the accident of birth would bring more legitimacy to the work of the second chamber: in turn, the chamber itself might then have the confidence to use its powers more robustly. Where the Commons is not widely held in high regard, and mainstream politicians often find television more useful to them than parliament, this would be a real plus for democracy. For democracy needs more than adversarial party warfare. Popular politics alone are not enough. As George Washington once said, 'Among civilised nations no state of government is in such disrepute as democracy. It leads to faction.'

Those who value the House of Lords should realise clearly that the second chamber would gain greater legitimacy through change. But they should also appreciate that this will entitle the Lords to exercise its powers more robustly. This is welcome. There would be no point in a facelift if the body were expected to remain frail.

CHAPTER FIVE

REFERENDUMS

By 2030 the chosen spokesmen of each political party will be able to address every voter as effectively as he can now address parliament. And so the electorate itself, rather than its representatives, may decide each vital political issue. After the spokesman of each part has had his (or her) say, the voters of the entire country could be recorded and counted by mechanism installed in the telephone exchanges. Within twenty minutes from the end of the last speech, the will of a national jury on any subject could be ascertained and announced.

(The Earl of Birkenhead, successively lord chancellor and secretary of state for India, in The World in 2030 AD, *1930)*

How should people participate in their government? Directly or by choosing representatives from time to time? Or by a combination of both? Since the seventeenth century, democrats have divided into two main schools of thought as to how the ideal of democracy should best be realised. The first is direct democracy. This was advocated by the Levellers under Cromwell, and by Jean Jacques Rousseau. According to them, the only truly democratic way to govern is by the full and direct participation of all citizens. The second contrasting line of argument favours representative democracy, as championed by John Stuart Mill and others. According to them, direct democracy can be achieved only in small political groups where the voting citizens can devote a considerable amount of time to political decisions, such as in the slave-operated Greek city-states. They argue that in the modern nation-state, where full and informed debate by the assembled citizens is impossible, representative democracy is the only way forward. It is this form of democracy that now holds sway in most of the countries around the world.

The referendum can nonetheless provide an additional direct contribution by the electors in these democracies. While not attaining the ultimate ideal of direct democracy, this strikes a compromise between the two extremes. On the one hand, the day-to-day government of the nation is conducted by elected representatives on a specific mandate for a set period of time. On the other hand, questions of vital national or moral importance can be decided by the electorate as a whole by means of a referendum.

Most democracies have at some time or other held referendums: of the major democracies only India, Israel, Japan, the Netherlands, the United States (as a whole nation) and the Federal Republic of Germany have never had a nationwide referendum. In most countries referendums have been used as opportunist affairs designed to solve a specific political difficulty. Governments may deem a referendum useful to help them avoid deciding a controversial political issue, or may find it convenient to commit themselves to a referendum on a particular issue in a general election manifesto. But in some countries, most notably Switzerland, Italy and some states within the US, referendums have become a regular pattern of governance. In states of the US, with California a notable example, there is often the opportunity to vote on 'propositions'. In Switzerland six to twelve national questions, typically spread over two to four ballots, are put before the people every year. In some countries, such as Australia and Ireland, they may be necessary to secure changes to a written constitution.

Referendums appear to be gaining popularity in democracies around the world. In the aftermath of the collapse of the Soviet Union, the referendum was used by many of the emerging democracies to legitimise the newly formed regimes and to demonstrate the break from autocratic dictatorships. So it is worth considering the past and potential future role of the referendum within the United Kingdom's constitution. Is it a desirable addition to our traditional representative form of government? And if so, how should it be operated?

Parliamentary supremacy is the cornerstone of the United Kingdom's constitution. So it is hardly surprising that in the past the referendum has not been thought to have much of a role to play. Politicians would not lightly surrender the task of deciding what is best for us. But even the most fervent and articulate advocate of that doctrine, Albert Venn Dicey, the last great nineteenth-century jurist, recognised that for vital, landmark issues there was a place for the referendum. For him a crucial weakness in the British system of government was 'the possibility . . . which no one can dispute of a fundamental change passing into law which the mass of the nation do not desire'. In Dicey's view, Gladstone's policy of Irish home rule was just such a change. So he advocated the use of the referendum: but less as a means of promoting popular participation, and more as a check on what he saw as the excesses of party-driven government. In other words, he became a convert because he feared parliament would decide the issue against his beliefs. Nonetheless he is still widely regarded as one of our greatest constitutional scholars, and his views help to legitimise the principle of the referendum. In his words:

> The referendum . . . is the one available check on the recklessness of Party leaders . . . and would lead to a formal acknowledgment of the doctrine which lies at the basis of English democracy – that a law depends at bottom for its enactment on the consent of the nation as represented by the electors.

Not long afterwards the suggestion of a referendum was raised again. This time the Conservatives were seeking to hold at bay the early-twentieth-century Liberal reforms which would reduce the powers of the House of Lords. They suggested that the referendum should be used to resolve a dispute between the two Houses in relation to any non-financial bill, and before passing any 'constitutional' legislation. If pursued, it would have raised the need to decide what was and was not 'constitutional' legislation. This is always a difficult task in a country without a written constitution.

The groundswell of support for referendums at the beginning of the twentieth century was considerable. The idea was put forward by several prominent figures as a means of solving the vexed question of tariff reform. In 1903 Joseph Chamberlain advocated its use. In 1910 Arthur Balfour thought the idea might be useful, and in 1930 Lord Beaverbrook suggested its use. In spite of this early recognition of the constitutional viability and benefits of the referendum, none was ever actually held at the time. But the idea took root.

In the 1930s the misuse of referendums in Europe discredited them in UK eyes. Hitler exploited referendums, so much so that they are not permissible under the modern German constitution. This abuse had happened before and has happened since. Napoleon I in France and General Pinochet in Chile were skilled exploiters of the art of shoring up their position by carefully phrased and stage-managed popular votes. When in 1945 Winston Churchill proposed that a referendum should be held on whether to prolong the wartime coalition, Clement Attlee, the Labour leader, protested:

> I could not consent to the introduction into our national life of a device so alien to all our traditions as the referendum, which has only too often been the instrument of Nazism and Fascism. Hitler's practices in the field of referenda and plebiscites can hardly have endeared these expedients to the British heart.

But, as time passed, the idea was revived and became a reality. In Wales people voted county by county on Sunday licensing laws, a splendid illustration of subsidiarity in action. The referendum was first used in part of the United Kingdom in the Northern Ireland border poll of 1973. The 1949 Ireland Act, which had given independence to the Republic of Ireland, had also provided that Northern Ireland would not cease to be a part of the United Kingdom without the consent of its parliament, Stormont. However, following the troubles in the early 1970s, Edward Heath's government prorogued Stormont and therefore had to find some other way to affirm the status of Northern Ireland. Heath promised that 'a system of regular plebiscites' would be held at ten-yearly intervals, and called the first in 1973. While it was hoped that this would 'take the border out of politics' in Northern Ireland, it was attacked by the Catholic republican parties as mere propaganda, given that Northern Ireland had been established in 1920 on the basis of its Protestant majority. In the event, 98.9 per cent of the 58.6 per cent who turned out voted in favour of continued union with Great Britain. Despite Heath's promise, no further border poll has been held to date. The Northern Ireland Constitution Act of 1976 nonetheless provides that Ireland shall not cease to be part of the United Kingdom without the consent of the electorate of Northern Ireland. This position has been confirmed by all UK parties in the recent peace initiatives.

The only national referendum that has ever occurred in the history of the United Kingdom's constitution was that held over Britain's participation in the European Community. As with the question of home rule, this issue split both major parties. Labour's left wing was reluctant to commit itself to what it saw as a capitalist cartel. The Conservative right wing thought that entry would undermine the Commonwealth and Britain's old imperial ties. However, in 1970, just before the general election, all three parties had supported British entry: so when Edward Heath secured agreement with the members of the community on the terms for British entry, the issue had not been fought out before the electorate. This decision to join involved the sharing of sovereignty, and accepting the supremacy of European Community law over our own. It was the most important constitutional change this century. The European Communities Act of 1972 provided for the dominance of European law. The European institutions were granted sweeping powers over our own. European law was to be interpreted by the European Court of Justice, an overarching court applying its own legal principles.

Despite all this, Heath claimed that no referendum would be necessary to ratify Britain's entry. The Labour party, concerned about a split within its ranks, took a different view. In James Callaghan's words it favoured the referendum as 'a rubber life raft into which the party may one day have to climb'. When Labour returned to power in 1974 it renegotiated the terms of Britain's entry, and put these to the people in June 1975. It also suspended the convention of collective cabinet responsibility. Politicians were allowed to campaign for their point of view across party lines. This, and the focus on the single issue, led to the best and most thorough arguments on a single issue ever put to our electorate. It was a compelling debate, deepening understanding of the issues, and conducted at a level which respected people's intelligence. In the end the referendum endorsed Britain's membership of the EC by a decisive majority of 67 to 33 per cent on a 65 per cent turnout. The argument had been truly influential. Not long before the referendum, public opinion was running two to one against Britain's continuing membership. The process of debate in the referendum reversed this position. The referendum was resorted to not as a system of fostering direct participation, but as a way of resolving the divisions within the Labour party. Yet its effect was to secure a thumping assent which legitimised our place in Europe and settled the issue of 'in or out', at any rate for twenty years.

But some were still curmudgeonly about the results. Enoch

Powell, a passionate opponent, explained it in these words: 'The fault does not lie with many of the advocates of British membership, who declared candidly that the nation-state was obsolete and that Britain therefore must become a province in a new European state and cease to be a self-governing nation.' This was an honest and blatant assertion of what politicians often think but normally conceal: that people are apparently too stupid to decide on their own interests, and the government has to decide what is good for them. In diametric opposition to the laws of the market, the producer has to decide what the consumer wants. Dumb and ignorant electorates cannot be safely trusted with their own destiny. This probably explains why politicians consistently insult the electorate with a combination of soundbites, attack their opponents and seek to avoid debating the tough issues. The EEC referendum showed how wrong this elitist attitude can be.

Once the principle was established, other regional referendums were held in the United Kingdom. The Labour government was forced by back-bench pressure to concede referendums on its proposals for devolution in Scotland and Wales. Once again, the referendum was being used as a device to avoid a split in the governing party. In the words of S. E. Finer, the referendum had become 'the Pontius Pilate of British politics', enabling MPs to vote for a bill while washing their hands of it. An amendment was introduced by George Cunningham, a Labour back-bencher and opponent of devolution, requiring 40 per cent of the relevant electorates to vote 'Yes' in a referendum before devolution could come into force. Thus not only were abstentions to count against devolution, but the lower the turnout of the electorate the higher the majority had to be that voted in favour of devolution.

The devolution referendums took place in March 1979, and resulted in defeat for both suggestions. In Wales, 59 per cent of the electorate turned out, an emphatic 80 per cent of whom voted to keep the existing system. In Scotland the result was more equivocal, with a turnout of 64 per cent, of whom 52 per cent supported devolution: only 32 per cent of the population had voted in favour of devolution and so the proposal failed.

In 1992 the issue of the referendum was once more canvassed when Denmark and France put the Maastricht Treaty to referendums for ratification. Many suggested that the Conservative government should do likewise. John Major declined, saying that the matter lay exclusively in the hands of parliament, whose will was sovereign. In any event the 'opt out' provision meant that the central issue of close political convergence and monetary union was effectively postponed to a later date. There was therefore, as he saw it, no 'live' issue to put before the electorate. But all three major political parties have now been pressurised into favouring the holding of a referendum over the vexed issue of monetary union, and the Referendum Party formed by Sir James Goldsmith wanted a wider, if much less focused, referendum on Europe. The Labour government has called a referendum on the issue of devolution in those parts of the United Kingdom for which devolution is contemplated. It promises further referendums on proportional representation and London local government.

So it is no longer true that the referendum is a strange continental device, entirely alien to our unwritten constitution. It has been with us in principle, if not always in practice, for over a century. It has been used, and used effectively, to resolve some of the most significant constitutional issues of the twentieth century. The time has surely come to consider whether its use should become more widespread. What are the potential advantages and disadvantages?

It is quite clear that referendums bring many benefits. As we have seen, the referendum forms a useful bridge between representative and direct democracy by increasing citizen participation on issues which fundamentally affect their lives. In a general election, the people are asked to vote on a range of different issues described in loosely worded party manifestos. No one can know for certain whether voters supported any particular manifesto commitment. By contrast, in a referendum a single issue is put to the electorate, and a specific and unambiguous answer is given.

Increased participation also brings wider, more informed and more detailed debate. Important decisions are reached only after the full soundings have been taken, and the electorate individually consulted. In giving each citizen a direct vote, each citizen is also given a voice. No interest or faction is left out. All are equally represented. In particular, internal party divisions, normally hidden behind the cloak of collective responsibility and by the clout of the whips, can be brought to light. Leading politicians are able to speak out on serious issues in an unclouded way. Michael Heseltine and Kenneth Clarke could, if they wished, join forces with Tony Blair and Gordon Brown to do battle with the Eurosceptics on whether we should join a single currency. Many commentators believe that this increased participation by people in decision-taking is a goal in itself. Benefits flow from people being aware of the issues in society beyond their immediate private concerns. People are now better educated, and are on average much more prosperous than they were. Working hours are shorter so that they have time, if they wish, to take an intelligent interest in public affairs. Radio, television and the Internet provide a revolution in the way in which the arguments can be communicated. Only a century ago we were limited to the great political rally and the newspapers. People who are allowed to take more of their own decisions become more mature, more responsible and less isolated. No longer can they just shrug their shoulders, turn on the latest television soap and blame the politicians.

The referendum enables the electorate to believe that it is they who ultimately govern. This is a central element to any democratic constitutional framework. Absolute monarchs such as the Stuarts traditionally justified their power by popular appeals to the divine right of kings. Even in the nineteenth century, Walter Bagehot recognised the importance of the monarchy in winning populist support for the government of the day. Today society is not so easily hoodwinked. If people feel that their interests are not consulted, or that they are not adequately represented, there is a resulting decline in societal stability. As Geoffrey Walker has observed: 'The citizen is more likely to feel entitled to flout a law promoted by an elite, or procured by blackmail or corruption, than one that is seen to reflect the free and informed consent of the majority of citizens.' But referendums, like any other forms of government, are not immune from criticism. Some criticisms are more cogent than others. One long-standing elitist objection is that they are said to promote decision-making by ignorant, uncomprehending voters. This was Bagehot's fear when considering the widening of the franchise in the nineteenth century. But even he recognised that such an objection could hold little sway in a literate and well-educated society, where modern telecommunications and access to information mean that the truly ignorant are few and far between.

Another traditional objection has been the social and economic costs of referendums. In Switzerland, where the referendum has achieved its greatest role to date, the costs of running campaigns range from between 500,000 to over a million Swiss francs (roughly £215,000 to £430,000), and Switzerland is a small country. If referendums become over-utilised there are social costs involved. Either ill-informed hasty decisions are made, or valuable time and money must be spent informing and consulting the electorate and debating the issues. But if referendums are used sparingly this objection loses most of its force. The costs are not too daunting, and they pale into insignificance beside the considerable economic and social benefits we stand to gain if government is able to carry genuine majority support for its most important and sensitive policies.

It is also said that a referendum, far from fostering direct participation, promotes apathy. Governments can avoid hammering out tough decisions and shirk difficult issues. The people may simply get bored. Experience elsewhere suggests that participation in referendums is generally rather lower than for elections where representatives are being chosen, but not greatly so. If an issue is important enough, and controversial enough, that the government cannot resolve it internally, why is it not better to consult the people?

Perhaps the most serious charge levelled against the referendum is that it runs the risk of promoting the tyranny of the majority over minority interests. Elected representatives are often ready to compromise minority interests to avoid alienating a large number of voters at the next election. Minorities can find it tough going in any form of democracy. After the last election, who can be said to represent passionately the bottom 20 per cent or so of our society? There is a current bipartisan belief among the two major parties, with only the Liberal Democrats standing for the contrary view, that taxes should not be raised to help the underclass. So the position of the disadvantaged might not be much worse if, say, the issue of whether taxes should rise to help some minority interests were put to a referendum. But media appeals to populist beliefs have often produced innately conservative results on social issues. They have generally favoured the *status quo*. In Australia, liberal reforms have rarely succeeded through the referendum process. In Ireland referendums have effectively vetoed the introduction of abortion and, until recently, divorce laws. This has led in Scandinavia to the rejection of the concept of the referendum as a tool for democracy. As Tage Erlander, Sweden's Social Democratic prime minister, said in 1948:

> It becomes much harder to pursue an effective reform policy if reactionaries are offered the opportunity to appeal to people's natural conservatism and natural resistance to change. The enthusiasm of conservative parties for the referendum system is thus certainly related more or less consciously to the fact that

it provides an instrument for blocking a radical progressive policy.

Ultimately this raises a question of who should govern: a civilised, liberal-minded elite or the popular will of the majority? This is the old elitist objection to the referendum in another guise, and it is ultimately met by the same answer. Provided that the people are adequately and fairly informed and the issues widely debated, and provided that politicians continue to play a prominent part in that debate, the fear of a conservative bias is no reason for declining to trust the will of the people.

There can be no certainty. Some of us, who are against capital punishment, take the risk that the vote of the people in a referendum would go against us. But why should it if the case is properly argued? With memories of the Guildford Four, the Birmingham Six and, most recently, the Bridgewater case, the argument that convictions may later be proved to be unsafe may well carry considerable resonance. It will be strengthened if it becomes accepted that, as some believe, James Hanratty was wrongfully hanged for the A6 murder some forty years ago. We should not lightly assume that our people are immune to arguments based either on civilised values or fairness.

For there is a constant danger that politicians underestimate the ability of the electorate to debate and determine issues of importance to all our lives. The soundbite arguments encouraged by the media, the instinct of politicians for not giving a straight answer to questions, the failure to debate an issue through, are all symptomatic of the tendency of government to underestimate the intelligence of the people.

I believe that the time has come for Britain to contemplate the establishment of a more permanent framework for using referendums. The best way to do this would be by legislation, laying down the procedures governing the initiation and conduct of referendums. This would need to clarify whether the outcome of such referendums would be advisory or mandatory, who would make up the electorate, when referendums should be nation-wide or regional, whether they would be subject to a threshold, as was the first Scottish devolution referendum, how the arguments should be communicated, how the campaigns should be organised, and how the polls should be held.

Many of the criticisms of the whole idea arise because of the way in which in individual countries a decision is taken as to which issue should be put to a referendum. If it is the people who decide it by petition, as in Switzerland and recently New Zealand, there is a risk that referendums are called haphazardly, that they become too frequent, and that representative government might fall into disuse. Government could all too easily be replaced by a system of excessive referendums and escalating costs, leading to populist, conservative and ill-thought-out suggestions for reform. The possibility of rejecting these proposed changes would not be a great consolation. Referendums need to be an occasional adjunct to representative government, and held only on important and controversial issues.

Where should the initiative lie within the framework of our constitution? In the few instances where referendums have been held in this country, the initiative has come from the government of the day. But there are strong arguments for saying that the initiative should not lie solely with government: it was specifically as a check on executive and party excess that Dicey favoured the referendum. Likewise, if the sole initiative were to lie with the Commons, it would be prone once again to party-driven loyalty and deployed by the whips. So it is perhaps important that there should be some filter. One possibility would be to put the decision in the hands of the constitutional commission which I have mentioned elsewhere as potentially making a valuable contribution to our democracy. This commission, drawn from both Houses of parliament and outside, could consider the seriousness of

the issue, the extent of the public and parliamentary controversy, and decide whether in principle a referendum should
be held, how the public could best be informed, and what the
question should be. Clearly if parliament as a whole had voted
for the referendum, then the commission would give effect to
this decision. But it would still have the role of ensuring that
the issue is put in the right way and setting out the ground
rules for the conduct of the campaign. In voting, say, for a
Scottish parliament or Welsh assembly, it is important that
voters should know what are to be the powers of those bodies
and how they will interact with the power of the Westminster
parliament, as well as whether the number of MPs in either
country should be reduced. This role of the commission would
start experimentally, but in the light of experience the ground
would become comparatively well trodden and there would
be precedents for future referendums.

For the whole of this century, leading politicians have been
getting used to the idea of referendums. A few have been held.
The results have been widely accepted, and have made a
significant contribution to the democratic process. Parliament
clearly has a large role to play in government. But there are
issues which cross party lines, or which divide society as a
whole, or which are fundamental to our future, where the
voice of the people should be directly expressed. A general
election campaign is no substitute. The standards of debate,
as in the shrill, spoiling, negative and largely policy-free campaign of 1997, are too poor and diffuse to enable people to
probe individual issues in depth. No one can be certain which
issues influence the electorate in their choice. In any event,
some issues which played no part in an election campaign
arise during the course of the life of a parliament. Momentous
issues deserve the full and informed involvement of our
people. They should no longer be limited to their occasional
opportunity to cast a vote for a representative member of
parliament. People are educated enough, mature enough, and
enough affected by the decisions of government, to be granted

a larger part in our democracy. The referendum should no longer be the exception to get a political party out of trouble. It should become an accepted way of taking the views of the people on issues which will shape their lives and those of their children.

CHAPTER SIX

DEVOLUTION

Rightly or wrongly, I am convinced that, if we wish to retain the unity of the United Kingdom, we shall be driven to set up subordinate legislative assemblies in Northern Ireland, Scotland, probably in Wales and, I would expect, in various parts of England.

(Lord Hailsham of St Marylebone,
The Dilemma of Democracy, *1978)*

While parliamentary reform is key to the health of democracy, the new Labour government has put devolution at the top of its agenda. It has introduced a short bill to enable referendums to be held in Scotland and Wales. The people of Scotland are to be given the choice of saying whether there should be a Scottish parliament, and if so whether such a parliament should have power to vary taxation. There are no details of how wide any such tax raising ability should be. The people of Wales are to be given the opportunity to decide whether there should be an assembly. In neither case does the intended legislation set out how the new bodies will be elected or appointed, or what the range of their powers will be, or what their relationship will be with the parliament in Westminster. Nor does the bill deal with the vexed issue of whether the number of members of the United Kingdom parliament from each country should be reduced. It is essentially to be the broadest general indication of principle without people being given the opportunity to know what the implications of the new system of government might be. This would have to be hammered out in parliament later.

No one can sensibly dispute the importance of grasping firmly the issue of whether the Scots or Welsh want more power over their own affairs. If they do then their wishes should be granted. But they should not be asked to buy a pig in a poke. To enable them to take an informed decision, the details of the proposals need to be worked through with care. If they are not, then the electorate are being denied the chance of exercising a balanced judgement when they are asked to vote. The present proposal carries dangerous and unnecessary risks if pursued with unseemly haste. These risks are compounded because the issue is being approached in the wrong order. For people to be asked to vote for a parliament without knowing for sure what sort of parliament they would get hardly does justice to their intelligence. The publication of a white paper before the referendum setting out draft proposals simply does not meet this difficulty. For we have no means of knowing which parts of the white paper will eventually become law.

Nor can devolution sensibly be considered in isolation from the powers and role of local government. In the next essay I argue strongly that local government should regain its role in our democracy. A Scottish and a Welsh parliament would add extra tiers of government. It is hugely important that devolution should not stand in the way of the powers of local government. It would be a bitter paradox if the recent erosion of local government led in turn to devolution and then on to total separation.

Devolution is not a new issue. It is more than 110 years ago that Gladstone as prime minister introduced his first Home Rule Bill for Ireland. In the same year the Scottish Home Rule Association, and Cymru Fydd, a society seeking a Welsh parliament, were founded. One hundred and ten years later the governance of Ireland, Scotland and Wales is still a topic prompting keen feelings and passionate debate.

Over the last few years intense efforts have been made to reach an agreement or understanding that might bring lasting peace in Ulster. Both the Labour and Liberal Democrat parties support some form of devolution for Scotland and Wales. Yet there are tough issues underlying the proposal which need to be thought through carefully before decisions are set in stone. Is devolution just a form of subsidiarity, passing power back to the people? Or would it lead to the break-up of the United Kingdom? What effect would it have on the representation of those areas in parliament? Would they be less well subsidised by central government? What would be the range of powers to be exercised in future by the new parliament and not from Westminster? Who would be liable for any new 'tartan tax'? How will that tax fit into the taxation policy of the UK? But, perhaps over and above all these, how much should we respect the wishes of peoples for self-government? Have we any right not to pass power back to the people, if they are prepared to accept both the advantages and disadvantages of taking responsibility for their own affairs?

The instinct of people to have a larger say in how they are governed is not new. But this instinct is heightened by the trend towards centralised power. This leaves many people and areas impotent, without responsibility for their own affairs, sceptical and critical of the way government is conducted, and with the firm belief that central government may care very little about them anyway. People become highly critical, yet they are at the same time denied the understanding which would come from wrestling with difficult and sometimes intractable problems. No wonder they can become apathetic about political issues. No wonder that the turnout at the last general election was only 70 per cent, and no wonder that only about 40 per cent of people vote in local elections.

In 1969 the Royal Commission on the Constitution was set up to examine 'the present functions of central government and government in relation to the several counties, nations and regions of the United Kingdom' to see whether 'any changes are desirable in those functions or otherwise in present constitutional and economic relationships'. The commission reported in 1973 that the widening dissatisfaction with government in the United Kingdom stemmed from the centralisation of government in London, or from developments in the operation of government which tended to run counter to the principles of democracy. These developments included the increased power of the executive, or, more particularly, whichever party happened to command a majority in the House of Commons. The commission found that the cumulative effect was that 'People have tended to become disenchanted with government. Their trust in it has been weakened. They are bewildered by it and are not confident that it is operating in a truly democratic way, responding properly to their own views and feelings.'

So the diagnosis was clear even before the condition was worsened by the increasing grasping of power by central government in the last twenty years. Local authority and responsibility have withered. The alienation, and the need for change, are now even more obvious than when the commission reported twenty years ago, particularly in Scotland. At the time there was already some wide cross-party support for devolution. The Conservative party held office nationally from 1979 to 1997, but the voters in Scotland and Wales regularly returned a majority of MPs from opposition parties. In a sense both these countries supported the opposition. In some ways nonetheless they did well out of central government. The subsidy per head to the inhabitants of Scotland is about £1,000 more per year than it is to those of Cornwall, although some Scots would argue that this fails to give them proper credit for North Sea oil. Each country has had its own minister and grand committee at Westminster to consider its affairs. It would be wrong to suggest that the last government had neglected either Scotland or Wales. But, for all that, some decisions at Westminster caused deep resentment and seemed insensitive. A glaring illustration was the imposition of the poll tax in Scotland one year ahead of the rest of the United Kingdom. Scotland has, then and at other times, seen itself as the pilot laboratory. In any event the peoples of these clearly defined regions, once independent countries, with their strong and ruggedly individual national heritages and cultures, are keen to have a greater say in deciding their own affairs.

So we cannot avoid the reality and depth of the emotion and conviction that something must be done to give greater self-government to these nations within the United Kingdom. What should it be? Of the various solutions canvassed by the politicians and the press, it is the issue of devolution that is most commonly seen as the ultimate panacea. Nor would the UK be alone if it were to take this path. Other countries, such as Spain and Germany with its division into local *Länder*, have shown that devolved or federal government can work. Another European neighbour, France, is seeking to pass greater power to the provincial government structure.

It is easy and seductive to talk about devolution in broad general terms. But the idea has at some stage to be worked out in concrete terms, and its consequences thought through. The devil is in the detail. There is no shortage of proposals, but they differ greatly. We have to define just what is meant by any proposal for 'devolution'. At one end of the spectrum there is outright separation. Scotland and Wales could become independent states, with their own independent executives and legislatures. At the moment this idea would appear to command negligible popular support in Wales, although significantly more in Scotland. An alternative possibility would be to introduce some form of federalism. Westminster could give up certain powers, retaining powers which can only be operated at a national level, such as defence, foreign policy and overall economic policy. This possibility shades into various kinds and degrees of devolution.

The Royal Commission on the Constitution identified three types of devolution. Legislative devolution would involve

Westminster giving full power to legislate in certain areas of government to an assembly. One way to do this is by listing the areas in which the assembly might legislate. Such was the approach of the devolution proposals which were drawn up by the last Labour government, and which were repealed in 1979 after a referendum in Scotland failed to gain enough support for devolution. Alternatively, Westminster could simply say what areas the local assembly might not legislate in. This is the method which has been favoured by the Labour and Liberal Democrat parties.

Secondly, there is what the Royal Commission called 'executive devolution', where responsibility for subordinate policy-making and administration is devolved to the assembly. Under this model Westminster would decide issues of general policy, and the assembly would then put them into practice. This is unlikely to find much favour. The traditional role of an assembly is to legislate and not to administer. Once the decisions are made they are best carried out by professional administrators. And, if the decision made at Westminster were unpopular, it would simply promote discontent and at best half-hearted compliance by the assembly.

The third kind of devolution identified by the commission is one where advisory or deliberative functions are given to an assembly. The Labour party's proposals for a Welsh assembly appear to fall into this category. Some may possibly welcome a talking shop about their own affairs, but I doubt whether people of real ability would be willing to take part for long. Such an assembly would quickly be seen as ineffective. It would certainly not give the people any more power over their own affairs. So in reality it would seem that only some form of legislative devolution would be of any practical value to the people claiming greater self-government.

Whichever method is chosen, there are other tough questions which cry out for a response. What voting system should be employed to elect the members of the assembly: first-past-the-post, or some form of proportional representation or a mix of electees and appointees from party lists? Can and should the powers of an assembly be 'entrenched', in other words protected from Westminster MPs changing their mind at a later date and taking back powers? Any government which has introduced a devolution bill in the past has quickly discovered the complexities of the issues raised.

There is an obvious temptation for those against the principle to set out the difficulties of devolution as a formidable obstacle, and these obstacles do need to be resolved if devolution is the wish of the people in Scotland and Wales. Yet we should be careful before we seek out clever arguments to resist the wishes of the peoples of the regions. For, if a people do want the power to govern their own affairs, then surely we should work out constructive ways for them to do so. It has long been recognised that there is no ground for denying a national grouping the right to self-determination. This is enshrined in the United Nations Covenant on Civil and Political Rights, which declares that 'All peoples have the right to self determination.' The same succinct and clear principle is reiterated in the UN Covenant on Economic, Social and Cultural Rights. This statement obviously begs the question of what the characteristics of a separate 'people' are. But few would deny that the Scots and Welsh are each a distinct 'people' within the United Kingdom.

Nor do we need to pore for long over the text of the statute of 1536 which provided that Wales was to 'stand and continue for ever from henceforth incorporated united and annexed to and with the realm of England', or over the Act of Union of 1707 with Scotland. In a democracy these solemn declarations simply cannot survive without the willing and continuing consent of all parties. The Act of Union of 1800 with Ireland, facilitated as it was by chicanery in the Irish legislature, failed to withstand this test almost from the outset. It had to be reversed and the consequences are still being painfully and slowly worked out.

There is one particular and fundamental difficulty which complicates devolution in the United Kingdom. In the United

States, Australia, Canada and Germany, the relationship between the states or provinces and central government is the same, so everyone across the country has the same opportunity to participate in democracy at both federal and local levels. This means that all members of congress have the same unquestioned entitlement to vote on national affairs. But in the United Kingdom there does not seem to be any possibility of agreeing on a single, coherent and balanced structure.

A parliament, possibly with tax-raising powers, is proposed for Scotland. An assembly with a more limited role appears to reflect the desire for devolution in Wales. In England, by contrast, or at least in large parts of England, there appears to be no substantial appetite for regional government as contrasted with stronger local government and more co-operation within and between the regions. It must be doubtful whether a United Kingdom with widely differing types of devolution would necessarily hold together for very long. It is likely that there would be constant dissent and dissatisfaction. There are powerful arguments that, to be workable, a system needs to be symmetrical, otherwise those with more power will be resented by those with less, while at the same time being tempted to claim yet more autonomy for themselves as an admittedly 'special case'. Nor is it obvious how England could be divided into regions without generating strong opposition. Take, for example, the south-west. This is one of the ten regional areas set up by the last government for administrative purposes. The south-west government region includes Cornwall, Devon, Dorset, Somerset, Wiltshire, Avon and Gloucestershire. Can it be said that inhabitants of, say, Swindon and Bodmin feel that they share a distinctive regional identity which could form the basis of a devolved region? Would Cornwall and Devon wish to be grouped together? From a glance at the map, the only possible division which might command any support and group together people who believe that they share a locality is the county division.

Even if we could find a coherent and balanced system of

devolution for the UK, there are inevitably a number of tensions and difficulties associated with devolution. Some have gone so far as to say that there is a fundamental inconsistency between the essence of our present system and any form of devolution. For example Enoch Powell has concluded that 'There is an inherent incompatibility between home rule, devolved legislative power and the maintenance of the parliamentary union in the United Kingdom.' We do not have to go to this extreme to recognise that there are major questions to be sensitively handled if we are to have a successful experiment in devolution.

The responsibility on those shaping and promoting devolution is the heavier because we have very little room for experiment. It is difficult to try out devolution on a small scale. Nor is it easy to do so in a way which allows the parties to return to previous arrangements if the new system does not work out well. There is no equivalent to cohabitation before marriage to see if a relationship is likely to be successful. Or, to put it another way, there is no question of a 'trial separation'. Many of those who have in the past opposed devolution for Scotland would say with Lord Younger, the former secretary of state, that if at least it is to be done, it should be made workable. It is also essential that people should know, as far as possible, what would be the precise powers of the assembly they are invited to vote for in any referendum. A vote on principle in a vacuum where there should be detail is not worth much. It is important that any means of devolution avoids the charge that it is imposed on the people from above and without their consent. People need at some time the opportunity to vote on the details of any proposed parliaments and assemblies if they are to be content with their powers. It is also important that in this process MPs should be free to represent their own individual views rather than being corralled into following the party line.

So what are the specific difficulties which might await us? Devolution risks challenging our sense of nationhood and

national community. It could undermine the general acceptance at a political level that we ought to have a common
interest in our common welfare. At present public policy and
the general social consensus assume that standards of welfare
and public services should be uniform across the nation. Areas
with greater perceived needs receive more than areas with
lesser needs. So there is no doctrine or accepted belief that
individual areas should only receive out of the public purse
in the form of public spending what they put into the purse
in the form of taxation. To a large extent our public finances
are managed on the basis of an attempt to provide for each
areas on the basis of its needs. Devolution and, in particular,
an unbalanced devolution giving more autonomy to people
in some areas that in others threatens this settled convention.

Proposals for devolution, and the practical experience of
devolution, would bring into sharp focus the tax revenues
generated by the various parts of the United Kingdom, and
the public spending allocated to those areas. These figures are
available now, of course, but they are not the subject of
vociferously critical debate. They show striking differences.
For example, identifiable public expenditure in Scotland was
some 24 per cent higher per head than in England in 1993–4.
The comparative figures for Wales and Northern Ireland were
18 and 40 per cent higher respectively. And these areas contributed less per head in tax revenues than England. There is
nothing necessarily wrong in principle with these marked
disparities in a united country. But if Scotland or Wales are
perceived as wishing to 'go it alone' and if a devolved assembly
clamours for greater financial support, then there will be
many who will begin to wonder whether they should not
'pay their own way'. Such a reaction might quickly generate
considerable popular support. People need to know of this
risk, and what it might cost them, before casting their vote to
lessen their links with Westminster.

We can also predict tensions over whether, and how much,
Scotland or Wales should pay towards public services which

are of general benefit to the nation as a whole but not of specific benefit to identifiable communities. Defence is an obvious example. Is there not a danger that an assembly could question whether it should contribute to such spending? This risk would be heightened if the assembly were dominated by a different party to that controlling the Westminster parliament. Once this happened, it might not be long before this assembly, and the people it influenced, were asking and indeed asked whether they wished to remain part of the United Kingdom at all.

The prospect that an assembly in Scotland or Wales would often be dominated by one party while another was in power in Westminster must also be clearly faced. Both Scotland and Wales have consistently returned a majority of Labour MPs to Westminster. At the general election in 1992, forty-nine out of a total of seventy-two members from Scotland were Labour. Of the thirty-eight Welsh MPs, twenty-seven were Labour members. After the 1997 general election there are no Conservative MPs at all in either Scotland or Wales. By contrast a Westminster parliament has often been dominated by the Conservative party. Such dominance would be more likely in future if there were to be a reduction in the number of MPs from Scotland and Wales, both to reflect their local autonomy and to reduce their influence over 'domestic' English legislation. The outlook for the relationship between the two levels of government in the long-term control of different parties is potentially bleak. This is vividly illustrated by relationships between Labour-controlled local authorities and Conservative-controlled central government over the years 1979–97. Recrimination and hostility, rather than co-operation, are a real risk and would sour relations.

There is also a European dimension. If there is a long-term dissonance between the party in control of an assembly and Westminster, then it is likely that the assembly will seek its own voice and representation in the European Union. It is also predictable that if Scotland, for example, is a net financial beneficiary of European Union funds, while England remains a net contributor to the European Union, Scotland will come under pressure to make a greater contribution to the English burden. These pressures may also lead to further separation between the two countries.

Not many people have wrestled closely with the detailed problems of devolution. Those who have done so realise that it is uncharted territory, and that we have no idea where it would lead in the end. The Constitution Unit's report on Scotland's parliament, *Fundamentals for a New Scotland Act*, published in 1996, and overall supportive of devolution, concludes with a studied understatement:

> Devolution to Scotland takes its place in a package of proposed reforms to the UK political system. It will in any event itself promote further change. It will open up to scrutiny parts of the political system which have remained relatively hidden to date: distribution of resources, of inward investment, of gains from European policies, and the attitude of Whitehall ministers and departments to Scottish issues.

The extent of the journey, rather like our entry into the European Community twenty-five years ago, cannot be easily predicted. Is it worth undertaking at all? That is one question which only the people of Scotland and Wales can answer.

There is one issue which those who are against devolution try to suggest is conclusive. How can Scottish MPs be entitled to vote on every question raised at Westminster after devolution, even on domestic questions which have no bearing on Scotland? This conundrum has been named the 'West Lothian question' after the long-standing MP for what was then the West Lothian constituency, Tam Dalyell, who has repeatedly raised the point in debates on devolution over the years.

There are currently seventy-two members of the Westminster parliament from Scotland. Should those members be entitled to vote on purely English issues, potentially overriding what would otherwise be the majority of English MPs? Should these same members, by contrast, not be able to vote on some of the very same issues which affect their own constituencies because those have been hived off to a Scottish parliament? Would Gordon Brown as chancellor representing a Scottish constituency be able to decide all English taxes but have no influence on the tartan tax? These conundrums indicate that the involvement of Scottish MPs would be a topsy-turvy one, able to intervene in English affairs but not in Scottish affairs.

The Labour party has so far sought to say that it is one more anomaly in a constitution full of inconsistencies, and so does not really matter. That attempt to brush a complex issue under the carpet is wholly unconvincing. But, for all the conundrums these issues raise, can it be right for opponents to chant that because they defy logic there can be no answer? For there is a clear precedent. When we felt the necessity of providing for a local parliament in Ulster, a solution was found. We did so by reducing the number of seats at Westminster allocated to Irish MPs. Obviously this answer is not conceptually perfect, and there were many fewer MPs from Ulster than there are in Scotland. But it is a compromise which has been accepted before, and could be accepted again if there were the will to respect any decision of the people of Scotland to have their own parliament.

The issues are nonetheless grave, serious and potentially permanent for the United Kingdom. There could be an increasing drift to fiscal independence, and gradually towards a wider independence of the countries making up the United Kingdom. It is on the cards that over time they would move towards complete separation. It is hard to see that such a momentous change is likely to be in the ultimate economic interests of any of the countries that currently make up the United Kingdom. Ironically, it was these very economic interests that led Scotland to cede independence in the first place as part of the Act of Union. So, accepting the right of the people to devolution, is there any alternative which can be positively considered?

It is hard to see much more that the central government can do on its own to meet the wishes of the people. Scotland, like Wales, but unlike the English regions, has its own specific member of cabinet. There are some 7,000 public servants within his department, which has a budget of almost £15 billion to spend on Scotland. This is significantly more per head of population than most other parts of the United Kingdom. The Scottish Grand Committee of members of parliament can consider issues which affect Scotland alone. But none of this has seemed enough to satisfy the appetite of people for their own government. Indeed, as we have seen, the electors of Scotland and Wales repelled the Conservatives at the last election more conclusively than ever before. And power must in the end, as is the central theme of these essays, be as close to the people as possible.

There undoubtedly are cogent reasons for decentralisation. Local cultures can exist and flourish within the structure of a broader political community. The European Union has so far proved a testimony to that achievement. The Gaelic languages are making a widespread comeback, and clansmen wear their tartan and celebrate Burns night, or at Murrayfield or Wembley when they get the right result, with justifiable pride. Yet, at the end of the day, cultural differentiation is not at the heart of the devolution debate. The return of the Stone of Scone to Scotland in 1996 may have represented a cultural triumph but it did not begin to satisfy people's aspirations. It was but the transfer of a symbol, and what Scots actually seem to want is more control over their own lives. The decentralisation debate is much more concerned with the devolution of executive and legislative power than cultural symbols. Guidance is to be found in the approach of subsidiarity. As with our relationships with the European Union, the concept of subsidiarity is one which can command popular support. The underlying principle is blindingly, devastatingly simple. Decisions should be taken as closely as possible to the people whose lives they affect.

This leads us to what is possibly the single real alternative to devolution as the way of achieving the goal of subsidiarity. If devolution is really concerned with the repatriation of overly centralised power, we should ask just what are the powers which are sought to be reclaimed. The usual answer, from both the people and the politicians, is that these should relate to issues such as revenue-collection, health, education and community interests. These are genuinely local issues, vitally affecting people's lives, where they want decisions to be sensitive to local needs.

But it is exactly these powers that were traditionally wielded by local government. The Royal Commission on the Constitution concluded that:

> The maintenance of a healthy system of local government requires that as many as possible of the functions of government which have to be carried out locally should be devolved to the local authorities, and that in the exercise of those functions the local authorities should be subject to a minimum of control.

It is interesting to note how closely this accords with the principle of subsidiarity. It accords, too, with the aims of those who seek devolution. Furthermore, building on the county-based system of local government would do much to answer the regional conundrum considered earlier in this chapter. If we were able in Scotland and Wales to build on the system of local government and to do so at the same time in England, that would give a much greater prospect of avoiding the fragmentation of the United Kingdom.

Ironically, far from promoting subsidiarity through local democracy, devolution and its local assemblies threaten to blur, confuse and further emasculate local government. John Patten, a former cabinet minister, has made this point forcefully:

> Walk into the streets or lanes of England, where there is two-tier local government, and ask a passing council taxpayer who

runs education or street cleaning. You will get the responsibility laid indiscriminately at the door of county or district council. Many local electors not only have that sense of confusion, but do not feel particularly close to the local authorities that are meant to serve them. This would be much worse if there was an extra tier inserted between local authorities and central government.

So a local assembly might add yet one more tier of government, distancing government from local communities. It would decide the more important issues for its regions. Local government might easily become little more than the local offices for the assembly. It would simply deliver services which had been decided upon and specified elsewhere. At very lowest, it would be hard to see how local government would be strengthened by the creation of regional assemblies. We need, if the impetus for regional government is not already irresistible, to pause and consider whether we should instead work to improve the existing devolved structure of local government so as to meet the highly legitimate concern about the centralisation of power. The emasculation of local government has taken power away from the people, away from the communities, and gathered it to a remote bureaucracy, governed by national politicians, who operate principally from London. Local government undoubtedly needs urgently restoring to health. In doing so, we might find a better, more well-trodden and less problem-fraught route than devolution to give people greater influence over their lives. We could apply the strengthening of local government uniformly across the United Kingdom. This would bring a better voice and influence to the people right across our communities, a real way of passing power to the people. It would mean the end of the West Lothian puzzle. When people are asked to consider local regional assemblies, with all their advantages and disadvantages, it is worth asking whether they would prefer strengthened local government with appropriate decision-taking, administrative and taxation powers. Power in other words to the grass roots and not to another, although more localised, form of central government.

The principle of self-determination which lies at the heart of devolution is fundamental to the rights of man. Calling a referendum is the only way to decide on such momentous questions. But intelligent people will want to know at some time what the powers of devolved government will be, what power there will be to raise tax, how much say their MPs will continue to have in the Westminster parliament, and how many of the powers of these devolved bodies could alternatively be discharged by local authorities. Not to offer the voters the chance to consider and express their views on these questions would risk sharp disillusionment in the future.

CHAPTER SEVEN

LOCAL GOVERNMENT

We have the most over-centralised government in the Western world.

(Tony Blair in the constitution debate;
Hansard, col. 1068, 20 February 1997)

We should welcome the more positive and sympathetic attitude of the current government to local government. Local authorities had become the unfortunate abandoned orphan children of our constitution – undernourished and starved of affection. We need to make sure that local government is restored to its rightful place, and that this is sufficiently entrenched and protected to avoid the danger of future governments eroding its powers anew. In other words we need to ensure that local authorities are readmitted as full members of our democracy. This is now overdue.

Local administration is one part of our government which truly does have a thousand-year history. In feudal times the great landowners gave protection and local justice to their people in exchange for allegiance and services. In Elizabethan times the central monarchy extended its power but placed the duty of policing and enforcing the poor laws on local communities. Shakespeare's cloddish but tenacious constables, Dogberry and Verges, had their key role in our rural society. So, too, did his Justice Shallow. Indeed for 600 years part-time, unpaid lay magistrates have been central to the administration of local justice. The 30,000 or so magistrates still try about 98 per cent of criminal cases, and hold local licensing, Youth and Family Court responsibilities. For most of this long history administration and justice could hardly have been other than local. Our country was covered by forests and the roads were rough and often impassable in winter. It was far harder to go from London to York than it now is to travel to Sydney. Communications, too, were rudimentary. Small communities generally bounded people's lives, as Laurie Lee reminded us in *Cider with Rosie*, describing life as it still was at the beginning of our own century. Even now there are still plenty of people living in Cornwall who have never travelled further than Plymouth.

But, in contrast to local administration, local democracy came much later. The timing of its development broadly mirrored the slow grant of the national franchise. In the nineteenth century, with the population growing and industrial towns and cities spreading rapidly, there was vital need for the work of elected local government. Joseph Chamberlain's three years as mayor of Birmingham in the 1870s were probably the most strikingly effective in the history of local government. The council under his leadership effectively nationalised at a local level gas, water and sanitation, and engaged in great slum-clearance schemes. Chamberlain raised the vision of the city with his belief that 'All monopolies which are sustained in any way by the state ought to be in the hands of the representatives of the people, by whom they should be administered, and to whom their profits should go.' His words strike a nostalgic chord, in a country of privatised water companies but afflicted by water shortage. He made the schemes commercial, so that they did not become a drag on the rates. He also ensured that the roads were surfaced, pavements laid, open spaces landscaped and museums created. His charismatic talents united the drive and commercialism of a skilled industrialist with the popular appeal of a demagogue.

Chamberlain was one of the few politicians who had first

built his reputation through local government. Many politicians since have served for a time on local councils. Indeed almost half of all members of the last parliament did so. A few gained prominence at local level, like Herbert Morrison in London and more recently David Blunkett in Sheffield. But most moved on promptly as soon as they got the first opportunity to step on to the national stage at Westminster. So there is no general ingrained reverence in central government for the part good local government should play in our national life. Contrast France, where President Chirac served as the mayor of Paris and where his first prime minister, Alain Juppé, was at the same time mayor of Bordeaux. Contrast the United States, where so many presidents have previously served as governors of their own states. Contrast Germany, where politicians often build their careers through being chief minister of their individual province or *Land*, and where Chancellor Kohl served as a member of the *Landtag* (state parliament) of Rhineland-Palatinate from 1959 to 1976, and as its minister president from 1969.

So in this country local government for the most part is but a stepping stone for ambitious politicians. They pay lip-service, perhaps for some of them even more than lip-service, to the constitutional role of local government. But what do they mean by this vague yet grandiose phrase? For local government has no sound and sure footing in our constitution. All power lies centrally, with our national government and parliament. Local government can in our country exercise only those powers which have been specifically conferred upon it by statute law. These powers are not entrenched, and can be altered or modified at any time at the whim of any central government which can command a majority in the House of Commons. There is no general power, as there is in many other countries, permitting local government a sensible, broad discretion to act for the benefit of their community. The nearest we have is Section 137 of the Local Government Act 1972 which does give a limited general consent for local authorities to incur expenditure where they have no other powers to do so. Their discretion is otherwise limited under Section 111 of the same act to the narrow category of acts 'conducive or incidental' to the discharge of the functions specifically permitted to them. But it does not extend the functions of local authorities, or give those local authorities power to determine the boundaries of their role, and the potential expenditure is now capped in a way to be calculated by central government. So it is no charter for a wide-ranging exercise of community leadership and vision.

But for all this some fine claims have been made for the strength of local government. In 1899, W. Blake Odgers, a leading historian of local government, wrote proudly:

> The parish meeting was the cradle in which our liberties were nursed. It was the school in which our forefathers learned those lessons of self-control, self-help, and self-reliance which have made the English nation what it is. Slowly and gradually they learned them, but by such lessons alone does a nation rise to a true conception of the meaning of liberty and the methods of self-government.

This Darwinian concept of the evolution of democracy was heady stuff, but it was long seen as part of the justification for local government. Sir Frank Layfield QC reminded us in 1976 that 'Local government has a value in its own right in promoting democracy; it acts as a counterweight to the uniformity inherent in government decisions.'

These high ambitions are not always easy to meet. Local government has a very wide-ranging role but it is often sedate, unspectacular work providing local services. Important policy decisions are, or so the perception goes, increasingly grasped by central government. In 1945 the responsibility for supplying gas and electricity was taken away from local authorities by nationalisation. In 1973 the provision of water and sewerage, which had long been regarded as one of the tasks of local government, was also nationalised. The shift to the centre had begun well before the tussle of the years 1979–97 between the Conservative government and Labour-led local authorities. But the flow of responsibility was not all one way. In a century in which the state has undertaken more provision for its citizens, the tasks delegated to local government grew markedly. Its scope includes the primary responsibility for planning, maintenance of streets, pavements and open spaces, provision of libraries, facilities for the arts, social housing, environmental issues such as pollution, refuse collection, education and the supply of social services. True it is that even some of these responsibilities have been taken away from local government in recent years: examples are polytechnics and higher education colleges, the careers service, and many direct services, where local authorities have been obliged to withdraw because of competitive tendering. In many areas, too, the local authority has become designated as the 'enabler' of services rather than itself providing the services directly. This of itself should not diminish the importance of local government. What the citizen wants is good service, whether provided directly or through competitive tendering. The local authority gains more respect by arranging for others to provide good services than by doing so directly and inefficiently or at too great an expense. The role of local government remains intensely important to any community and for most people has a far greater direct impact than that of central government. Budgets, too, have grown across the century to reflect the increased range of the responsibilities of local government. The total spend has risen from £75 million at the turn of the century to around £75 billion. Even after allowing for inflation the growth amounts to over 2,000 per cent.

Despite this, few people would say that central government had actively fostered the development of local government over the last twenty years. Before then there seemed to be a broadly harmonious mutual respect between central and local government as to the balance of responsibilities. The local government budget grew steadily. But by 1975, with the national finances at a low ebb, the position changed. Anthony Crosland, as secretary of state for the environment, famously declared: 'The party's over.' In 1979 the incoming Conservative government wished to take a grip on public expenditure. So it was concerned to clip the wings of local government spending. It did so first by seeking to taper the rate support grant so as to reduce the proportion paid by central government when a local authority exceeded what was judged to be its proper spending level. Each year there were legal challenges to these decisions, in the form of judicial review. It was argued that central government was acting outside its powers, or without properly considering local representations, or wholly unreasonably. Since local government has no entrenched constitutional role, there could be no other wider and more general constitutional challenge to these changes. Each year in the light of the legal challenges, which almost invariably failed, the government pushed new legislation through parliament. In 1984 rate-capping was introduced. Before that, the local authority could spend as it liked, if it was prepared to accept losing a proportion of the central government grant and justify its conduct to its own electorate. The limits set by rate-capping forbid the local authority from going beyond the centrally set spending limit even if its electorate approves. It quickly became a stick with which local authorities could beat the government. They could claim that any inadequacy in their services was caused not by their own incompetence or prodigal spending but by a refusal of a remote and unsympathetic central government to allow them to raise the funds necessary for their community. In some cases these complaints were justified, but by no means all.

So downright hostility developed between many in local government and the national government. Some local authorities set out to go beyond their local roles and challenge the central government. They not only overspent, but they formulated their own foreign policy, for example over the conduct of relations with Nicaragua or their defence policies of 'nuclear-free' zones, and sought to act as national oppositions on a local scale. Some thought their role extended to local sanctions on those, such as a rugby club, who dealt with South Africa during the apartheid regime. Not surprisingly central government in its turn reacted strongly to this counter-provocation. In some cases it overreacted, as when it abolished the Greater London Council in 1986. At no stage have Londoners supported this decision. At the time of abolition, 74 per cent of Londoners responded to a poll demanding the restoration of an elected body of some sort 'to govern London'. A decade later the British Market Research Bureau found that the figure remained exactly the same, and included Conservative as well as Labour voters. Simon Jenkins has rightly commented: 'There appeared to be an instinctive bond between the inhabitants of a city and the democratic process.' London is probably the only great capital in the democratic world which does not have its own elected governing body to co-ordinate action across the city. The consequences for local democracy in London have been totally retrograde. A hundred years ago Londoners elected 12,000 citizens to serve on councils, boards and committees. These ran the health, education, welfare and transport necessary for a great capital city. Now almost the same number of people still sit on boards administering local services in the capital. But the difference is that only slightly under 2,000 of them are elected. There is no single governing body for London, and no elected mayor who can campaign for the capital, although the new Labour government is committed to giving Londoners the choice by holding a referendum.

The dramatic reduction in the number of those elected to serve in the capital reflects the growth of the modern quango. The removal of services to non-elected bodies, together with the reduction in the freedom to budget, has been seen as another turn of the screw and has demoralised local government. Central government has taken control. It has moved powers and functions away from elected local authorities.

It is tempting to see this retreat from democracy as wholly retrograde. But in fact there is a strong argument for the existence of many of these appointed bodies. They can bring into the government of schools, or into bodies concerned with training, housing, urban development or higher education, people with business skills and specialist talents who create a wider mix of experience, and so contribute to higher standards and greater efficiency. These bodies can sometimes respond more specifically and sensitively to the needs of the interested consumer. But there are problems nonetheless. How should such quangos be appointed? To what extent should they be ring-fenced to avoid appointments becoming a reward for those supporting the political party in power? To whom should they be accountable? Should there be an element of local election? How should they interact with the local authority where both are involved in the same area of activity? Above all, how can the individual quangos take a wide view of the needs of a particular area?

Some of these questions are very hard to answer. But they should not stop us recognising the value of some of the changes of recent years. Council tenants have gained the right to buy their own homes, with all the encouragement this brings to take responsibility for and improve their condition. Local authorities are selling housing to the housing associations. Tenants seem to have a higher regard for housing associations than they do for local authorities. Individual tenants can have more influence and the opportunity of having their concerns listened to. Housing associations can be much more focused and specialised in their work precisely because they do not have the range of other operations that a local authority has to manage. Where tenancies are still with local authorities, the tenants now also have the 'right to manage'. They can take control of the management of their homes through a 'tenant-management organisation' if this is supported by enough tenants in a ballot. They can show more initiative and responsibility in carrying out improvements to their homes, and they can claim a proportion of the cost when they move. All this fosters individuality, a sense of responsibility and pride, and takes away the dead hand of monolithic local authority control.

In the same way education has been freed up so that there can be more individual management at a true local level. Schools which become 'grant-maintained' receive their grant directly from central government. While these are still only a small proportion of schools, it is nonetheless a step towards responsibility at the grass-roots level. So, too, is the devolution of most of the education budget from local authorities to schools and their governing bodies. Schools can decide how to spend their budget, and they can select their own staff. Over 90 per cent of the school budget is now delegated by local education authorities. All this reflects a policy that schools should carry out functions for themselves wherever possible. It is an exciting example of true subsidiarity in action.

Like all change, it has its teething problems. Teachers were not trained to be accountants. They need help in budgeting for their responsibilities in curriculum development and school management, and the support and commitment of governors with legal and accountancy skills. Devolution, too, can lead to the loss of centralised purchasing power, whether it be for school books or teachers' insurance. But the overall approach enhances both individual choice and responsibility. It may lead to despair if the overall budget is inadequate, but this in turn raises the pressures on government.

For wherever decisions can be delegated to the level of an individual school or housing association, the citizen becomes less remote from government. Is it not better that control should be handed over to those who are directly interested and affected? Certainly this approach has popular support. In 1994 an opinion poll recorded that only 38 per cent of those interviewed thought that local authorities should run schools. Only 27 per cent thought that local authorities should run local hospitals. So the role of local government is not immutable, and should be always evolving and changing to match the needs of society. Wherever possible it should be providing broad local leadership and strategic focus and withdrawing from direct services. In this way it can be both more responsive to the needs of its area and concentrate more tightly on securing efficiency in the delivery of services. If central government ought to devolve functions to local authorities, by the same token so local authorities ought wherever possible to devolve those functions to local organisations active in specific areas.

Other welcome changes have placed great emphasis on transparency, on communication and openness from local authorities. Communication is notoriously difficult. The message has to be spelt out and emphasised. But greater openness can undoubtedly help to spark more local understanding and participation and diminish the feeling of remoteness which people often feel. Members of the public now have the right to attend all council and committee meetings. They can have access to agenda reports, background documents and minutes. All the accounting and financial documents of local authorities, including their contracts and their bills, have to be available for public inspection once a year. The results of the audit must be published. Council tenants have to be sent annual reports including details on overall rent arrears, repair priorities, housing allocation and vacant properties, and the average weekly management cost per home. The Citizens' Charter obliges local authorities to meet performance standards and to publish details of how far these were achieved. Figures must, for example, be published on the percentage of street lights which are not working. This greater openness is a key part of accountability. It can promote the understanding of individual members of the community, and can help them act as a spur to accountability.

So I believe that recent history of local government has not been just a one-way street to centralisation. There has been much change designed to make local authorities more directly accountable, to devolve power down to individual units and to require local authorities to contract out services whenever that is more efficient. All this was very necessary. But it leaves its own problems. The accountability of some of these local bodies needs to be improved. There is no clear demarcation line between the overall responsibility of local authorities and the individual responsibility of appointed governing bodies. Most decisions for change have been made pragmatically. There is no underlying principle as to what local authorities should do, or how, if at all, the appointed bodies with individual management tasks should account to the wider community. The quangos are now responsible for over £30 billion of public spending. Central government appoints no fewer than 40,000 people to non-elected bodies. So there may be good management, but it is at a far greater distance from democracy. Openness is admirable, but it is not enough. There must be accountability, not to government in Westminster, but to the local community.

What was the effect of all this change taken together? Undoubtedly local authorities felt for some years under direct assault from central government. Many believed, as a House of Lords select committee recently reported, that they had been 'crushed and abused' by central government. Local authorities felt that they had less of a role, and so a diminishing number of good people wanted to play any part in local affairs. The select committee concluded:

> If . . . nothing is done very soon to strengthen the position of local government, there is a danger that it will be allowed to wither away from sheer neglect. While no central government is likely to abolish local government, there is a risk of a continued attrition of power and responsibilities away from local government until nothing meaningful is left.

The warning is timely. What can be done?

The esteem in which local government is held undoubtedly needs enhancing. For years the government refused to sign the Charter of Local Self-Government framed by the Council of Europe. Twenty-one other European countries, from both inside and outside the European Union, had no such hesitation. The charter is a splendid affirmation of the value and status of local government which when adopted would have the effect in the UK of putting it on a real footing of constitutional principle. Its broad underpinning includes the belief:

- that the local authorities are one of the main foundations of any democratic regime;
- that the right of citizens to participate in the conduct of public affairs is one of the democratic principles that is shared by all member states of the Council of Europe;
- that it is at local level that this right can be most directly exercised.

So the charter rolls on, stressing that local authorities should have the right and ability 'to regulate and manage a substantial share of public affairs under their responsibility and in the interests of the local population'.

Importantly, local authorities elsewhere in Europe are not to be fettered as they are in this country by the doctrine that confines them, and confines them only, to those powers which have been specifically granted. Quite the reverse is true. They have 'full discretion to exercise their initiative with regard to any matter which is not excluded from their competence nor assigned to any other authority'. They are allowed to exercise their powers with regard to local circumstances. They are entitled to be consulted in strategy planning on issues which directly affect them. The whole charter is a ringing assertion of the importance to people of local government. While in their final years in office the last government stepped back from a confrontational and adversarial approach, and agreed

some guidelines for consultation, they never committed themselves enthusiastically or wholeheartedly to the real value of
local government. But this commitment is badly needed. In a
country where politicians so obviously attach more importance to strutting upon the national stage, it is vital that as a
society we should demonstrate emphatically how vital it is
that local government should continue to have an important
and valued role. The government have now accepted the
charter. So it can become a touchstone of principle against
which proposed changes in the role of local government can
be tested.

That notable commitment obviously needs reinforcing by
other measures designed to give local authorities more
command over their own affairs. They need to be freed from
the shackles whereby they can only act under specific powers
granted by parliament. In this way, local authorities could be
able to shape policies for their own community. They also
need greater control over their own finances. Almost 80 per
cent of local government finance now comes from central
government. This finance is provided according to formulae
called Standard Spending Assessments. These are attempts to
ensure that payments are broadly equalised according to the
needs of particular localities. But inevitably, and complex as
they are, they cannot allow for all differences in individual
circumstances nor in the individual wishes of a particular
community. How can the balance be changed? One way
would be to return the non-domestic or business rate to the
control of local authority. In 1990 this had been taken to
central government control because it was felt that taxes on
business were charged at inequitable and divergent rates
across the country. But there seems little risk in the present
political climate that many local authorities would seek to
discourage business by punitive taxes and drive them to locate
elsewhere. In any event, this could be guarded against by
ensuring that local business should not be required to pay
more than the full cost of services it received from local

authorities. This might be hard to measure precisely, but attempting to do so would be a salutary discipline. What is absolutely essential is that local authorities should have the full opportunity to raise their own funds, from their own community. This above all would help make them more accountable to their local electorate. To buttress this accountability, rate capping should be abolished. A borrowing cap is worthwhile to prevent authorities piling up debt for their successors, but a spending cap is not. In a mature democracy local communities responsible to their local people should be able to decide what taxes they raise. If they overburden the people, then it will be demonstrably seen as their responsibility.

But, it may be said, we have been here before and local authorities abused their freedom. In some cases they did. But it has always been recognised that there can and ought to be a check on the power of local government. This is the role of the district auditor. Some may have the impression that the district auditor was created by Mrs Thatcher's government as a brigade of shock troops to bring local authorities into line, and that surcharges were created for Derek Hatton and his comrades in Liverpool. Not so. The post of district auditor dates back to 1879, and more than a century ago he was rooting out all sorts of quaint malpractice:

> In one parish a sparrow-shooting club for the farmers had for five and twenty years been supported by the highway rate. ... Among other items of disallowed expenditure we find champagne and plovers' eggs, visits to the theatre, journeying expenses when no journey was taken, presentation portraits, 'suitable demonstrations' on the Chairman's wedding day, memorial keys and the like.

The district auditor had then, as now, full power to disallow items and to surcharge those who directed illegal or improper payment with the amount of the sum which was misspent. This is a heavy penalty. It is not just a fine. It is currently the ability to pursue councillors to their last coin for recovery of money spent in breach of their fiduciary duty. Even if modified as Lord Nolan suggests to a common law offence of misconduct in a public office, the potential sanction will be strong. If local government were freed from some of its current shackles, this power would be there to guard against excesses. The district auditor could monitor if the business rate were being fairly charged. If some reserve power of capping were still thought to be necessary, it could be imposed by the district auditor to reflect the misspending of any authority which clearly stepped outside the line of what was a reasonable discharge of its local duties.

So in a mature democracy local authorities should have greater power. Undoubtedly there have been abuses in the past, there has been provocation as they sought to set up some policies well outside the usual range of local affairs, and all would not be perfect in the future. Nor will it be in central government or any other institution known to man. But we cannot expect mature conduct from local authorities, nor able people taking a part in their own affairs, if they do not have a really worthwhile role in their area. We should grant them this, with the district auditor in the background. Local government's need for a massive regeneration of authority is vividly demonstrated by the lack of interest which the electorate shows in the conduct of their local affairs. The percentage of the electorate which votes in local elections is low. It has for a long time stood at about 40 per cent. This was so before the erosion of power of recent years and reflects a more deep-seated lack of appreciation of the importance of local government. The lack of interest contrasts with France and Germany, where the turnout is typically 70 per cent of electors.

What is the reason for this apathy? Is it that the provision of services in a quiet way is an activity about which people grumble if it goes wrong but do not appreciate their power to influence? Or is it that in an age of wide opportunities people want to make their contributions in other ways? Successful businessmen may buy football clubs. Some people may want to engage in specific activities, such as serving as a school governor or trustee of a charity. Some people may care passionately about single issues like the environment, or homelessness, or their place of religious worship and want to make their input through their particular interest group. With all the width of entertainment and leisure activity, taken together with the other pressures of life, influencing local government may come low down the list. But surely there is another and much more concerning explanation. Local government has not been properly valued, not been nurtured by national government, not been raised to centre stage as a vital aspect of our society. People need to appreciate its importance if they are going to play a vigorous part in elections. This is why it is so important to raise constitutional significance by signing the European charter. It emphasises the need to treat local authorities as mature and influential democratic bodies, with the ability to plan widely for their own community, to have a significant say in their budget and to co-ordinate local activities in partnership with the appointed bodies. Communities should be able to shape their own government to meet what they see as individual needs. People should be able to choose whether they wish some form of proportional representation for their area. This could be decided by putting the issue to a local referendum. This could prevent the prospect of one party being in power and creating a mini-state with the attendant danger of corruption. The profile of local government needs to be raised, as does understanding of the immense contribution it can make to community and individual lives. People must be drawn into having a say in how their affairs are conducted. Greater communication, more participation and more freedom of local choice might all encourage an awareness that local democracy is precious. Perceptions would not change overnight. But there is a gap in our society. Local authorities are steadily diminished if the people of our communities are not committed to local democracy. The reversal of their decline is a vital task.

How, too, does all this relate to devolution? Local authorities serve across the length and breadth of the United Kingdom. This is not just an issue for particular countries, such as Ireland, Scotland or Wales. It is an issue for all of us. But if local government were strengthened, if its role were fully appreciated, and if people participated, then the voices seeking devolution might be more muted. For as Dr Jonathan Sacks, the chief rabbi, wrote in his passionate book, *The Politics of Hope*:

> A new style of politics . . . would seek, wherever possible, to increase participation in public life. To do so it would engage in a policy of decentralisation, handing back power to local bodies and self-governing institutions, understanding that the loss in central control is more than compensated by the civic good of participation.

There would be much to be said for enhancing the status of local authorities before putting the devolution issue to the vote. But devolution or no devolution, the strengthening of local government and the chance for our people to participate in their own community is still fundamental to achieving better government. Stronger local government would get rid of many grievances, lessen the perception of remoteness, and avoid putting a new, untried and unpredictable extra layer of government in post. We would avoid piling bureaucracy on bureaucracy..

CHAPTER EIGHT

EUROPE

I think that among peoples constituting geographic groups, like the peoples of Europe, there should be some kind of a federal bond. ... Obviously this association will be primarily economic, for that is the most urgent aspect of the question. ... Still, I am convinced that this federal link might also do useful work politically and socially, and without affecting the sovereignty of any of the nations belonging to the association.

(Aristide Briand, French foreign minister,
in a speech to the League of Nations in 1929)

Europe. The very word provokes the most passionate, and often shrill, political arguments of our time. In one sense this is surprising. Europe is after all not the most vital matter which people see as affecting their everyday lives. The economy, law and order, education, health, the environment in which we live, and our local services – all these are seen as having a more immediate and tangible impact on our lives. This is just as true for the peoples of France, Germany and the other countries in the European Union.

But there are a few, a very few, issues passionately fought out in their day which really do shape our country's future for a long time to come. The dissolution of the monasteries and the coming of Protestantism in Tudor England. The struggle between king and parliament in the seventeenth century. The growth of our empire, which marked the next 200 years. The gradual coming of democracy in the nineteenth century.

The long-running debate about free trade versus protectionism, which split the Conservative party over the Corn Laws and was again being fought out when in 1905 it brought gradual disintegration and electoral disaster to Balfour's Conservative government. Today the modern Conservative party is deeply and stridently split over Europe.

Our relations with continental Europe seem to me to be one of these rare momentous issues. They have already been a dominant theme for almost half a century, they are as yet unsettled, and their outcome will profoundly influence our future. One prophetic voice had realised this even before the last century ended. Lord Salisbury, the last prime minister of Queen Victoria's reign, said a hundred years ago: 'The federated action of Europe is our sole hope of escaping from the constant terror of war, which weighs down the spirits and darkens the prospect of every nation in this part of the world. The federation of Europe is the only hope we have.' His words were echoed by the founding fathers of Europe. But not before our century had experienced some of the darkest days of its history: two world wars costing more than sixty-five million lives, the tramping feet of invaders – in some cases twice, as in France – and the genocide of the Jews. All this was punctuated by an uneasy truce and prolonged economic depression.

So it was hardly surprising that some visionary European statesmen set out to try to avoid further conflict. We should never forget that this was the clear and predominant aim of the architects of the European Community. The preamble to the 1957 Treaty of Rome states that the founding nations are coming together 'to preserve and strengthen peace and liberty'. No longer was a single nation to be able to secure its future and prosperity by imperialism. Instead, countries were to bind themselves together by mutual self-interest. This meant that sound economic development had to be the basis of the new community. So they initially concentrated on the creation of a common market.

And what, at that time, of Britain? We were, as indeed were the other countries, to a large extent prisoners of our history. The history of our European neighbours led them to seek unity. Our history had been notably different. We are an island, and a world-wide trading nation. We had a large, if diminishing, empire, and, as we thought, a special relationship with the United States. But we did not realise that our role as a world power was draining away. With our geographical and historical links with Europe, we had inevitably been drawn into their conflicts across the centuries. Yet we had a suspicion of long-term involvement. George Canning, as foreign secretary not long after the Napoleonic era had ended at Waterloo, had resisted attempts to become involved 'deeply in all the politics of the Continent, whereas our true policy has always been not to interfere except in great emergency, and then with commanding force'.

This was the simplicity of a bygone age at the height of the Pax Britannica. The idea lingered on, although times changed. So it is not surprising that we were initially to stand aloof from the modern search for stability and union. In 1946 in a celebrated speech in Zurich, Sir Winston Churchill actually urged the establishment of a United States of Europe, to be based on a partnership between France and Germany. But the role which he saw for the United Kingdom was that of a friend and sponsor of the new Europe. Both Labour and Conservative governments were lukewarm and sceptical about Europe. Sometimes our concerns were imprecise, as when Ernest Bevin, as foreign secretary, used this startling mix of metaphors: 'I don't like it. I don't like it. If you open up that Pandora's box you will find it full of Trojan horses.'

So when the European Community was planned in 1955 we wanted no part of it. But we soon realised our mistake. The common market became a success. Only a few years later, with Harold Macmillan as prime minister, we made an abrupt about-turn and applied to join. This was because, as Macmillan put it, 'Through membership this country would not only gain stature in Europe, but also increase its standing and influence in the councils of the world.' We were not at first welcome. We had to make several applications to join, which emphasised the mistake we had made in staying out. By 1966 Harold Wilson is said to have told his cabinet that our economy was no longer viable on its own. But we had to wait until 1973 to join. It was our first experience of coming late to the party, and having to fit in with the arrangements which others had made. These included the perverse economic effects of the common agricultural policy, which are obstinately still with us today and with little prospect of improvement in the short term.

Long though we agonised over whether to join the European Community, we had already acknowledged the importance of continental links in other ways. We had from its inception played, as we continue to do, a strong part in NATO, which remains important in spite of the end of the cold war. It is a substantial sharing of sovereignty and a major commitment. If, for example, Iraq were to invade Turkey, we would go to war. It looks as if NATO will evolve to embrace at least some of the countries of central Europe. We must also assume that the United States will expect us gradually to make a greater contribution to our own defence and security. Firm co-operation between this country, Germany and France will be crucial to the successful enlargement and increasing Europeanisation of NATO. This is a key area of common interest, increasingly reflected in the way that the three countries co-operate in buying defence supplies.

We have also signed the European Convention on Human Rights. The convention, which is similar to a wider United Nations declaration, had its well-spring in the atrocities of the last war. It is designed to protect against arbitrary arrest, to ensure fair trial, to protect property, to secure privacy and to entrench the freedom of the press. Our citizens, and those of other countries, can bring claims that their rights have been infringed before the European Court of Human Rights in

Strasbourg. The convention, even though for many years governments declined to incorporate it into our own law, has nonetheless become in practice our most important modern constitutional document. It has a particularly important role in protecting minorities in an increasingly pluralist society.

There could hardly be two more vital aspects of life than defence and the protection of our fundamental rights. In both areas we have long recognised that we are part of Europe. But entry into the European Community was the most important watershed of all, for it radically affected our national sovereignty. It meant that we were prepared to share sovereignty with our mainland European partners in the areas of community activity. This in turn meant that we were prepared to accept that community law should become part of the law of this country and, further, that it should prevail over our own domestic law in cases of conflict. We accepted the jurisdiction of a second European court, this time sitting in Luxembourg. These decisions were taken by our own parliament, but were later confirmed by a referendum in which almost all serious politicians accepted that our future lay in Europe.

Or so we thought until fairly recently. But increasingly, and at a pace which has quickened dramatically over the last year or so, support for the European Union has seemed to dwindle. Some of the criticism was pretty unattractive stuff, jingoistic and fuelled by a distaste for foreigners. But there is also a growing Euroscepticism among many intelligent politicians, economists and writers. Even after the change of government and its welcome alteration in tone towards Europe, there is still nothing approaching the total and unquestioning approval of the aim with which John Major assumed office in 1990 to put this country 'at the heart of Europe'. All this raises ringing constitutional questions. Should we share our sovereignty with Europe at all? Or should we deepen our commitment as part of our involvement, integrating more of our activities? Would this strengthen our national influence in an age of globalisation?

Why has this change of sentiment come about? What are the cries of the doubters? Much of the fire is directed at the activities of the European commissioners. The central bureaucracy of Brussels seems to many to be remote, to be *dirigiste* and over-intrusive. One of the latest examples is the working time directive, aiming to decide what hours can be worked by employees in this country, and with what breaks and lengths of holiday. The European Court of Justice in Luxembourg is seen as centralist, upholding directives of this kind but at the same time failing to stop the 'quota-hopping' of Spanish fishing fleets which had bought UK companies in order to increase their quota by taking up some of our share of European fishing rights. The economies of some European countries appear weighed down by uncompetitive social charges and the inflexibility of their labour structures. This is contrasted with the increasing strength and job creation in our own United Kingdom economy. Our people understandably still see themselves as primarily citizens of our own country with its strong national culture and loyalty. Yet, so the argument runs, there are some headlong federalists in Europe who appear to want ever more political and economic integration whether over currency, fiscal policy, immigration, border controls, relations between employers and employees, or in the health and social field. The sceptics see these agendas as irreconcilable and say it is time to cry halt and surrender no more sovereignty. Indeed some say it has gone too far already. What is not in doubt is that this country has to make a fundamental and permanent choice.

Sir Nicholas Henderson, an ex-ambassador to three European countries and to the United States, neatly focused that choice when he recently wrote: 'The fundamental European question for Britain is: Will the outlook for present and future generations – their welfare, security, and the opportunities for a full life – best be served by participating in the creation of a closer European union; or is there an alternative?' The issues raised by this apparently simple question are complex and wide-ranging. They are in part practical, economic, cultural, instinctive, and they are in large measure constitutional. For our major constitutional development of the last forty years has been the gradual deepening involvement with what is now the European Union. It began with our signature of the Treaty of Rome in 1972. Britain's 'splendid isolation' or self-imposed quarantine came to an end. The implications of this, and its effect upon the say people have in the way they are governed, are among the most important issues we face as we approach the next millennium.

Just what has membership of the European Union meant for our constitution? It has influenced us at three levels: politically, legally and economically. When we joined Europe at the beginning of 1973 we unequivocally relinquished part of our sovereignty to the European institutions. Within the European Union there are four main political institutions: the council, the commission, the parliament, and the European Court of Justice. The council consists of ministers from each of the member states. It is the principal decision-taking body. The commission, which is often thought of as the centralist driving force, consists at the moment of twenty members, mostly former national politicians, appointed by the governments of the member states. The European Court of Justice comprises fifteen judges. There would normally be one from each state and one extra and they are formally appointed by the 'common accord' of the member states. Only the European parliament is directly elected and so directly accountable to the people of Europe.

But the powers of that parliament are limited. Its effectiveness has not so far been wide, and in this country people have little interest in its activities and do not see them as vital to their lives. Traditionally its role has been little more than a consultative one. Generally legislation is initiated by the commission, and then fed to the council and the parliament for consideration and (non-binding) comment, before the final form of the legislation is approved by the council. Some attempt to redress this 'democratic deficit' was made by the Single European Act and the Maastricht Treaty, which introduced a new 'co-decision' process: this allows the parliament to veto a proposal to which it remains opposed after all the necessary consultation has taken place, provided it does so by an absolute majority of all MEPs. However, this new procedure is not yet applied to all community legislation, and in some instances the European parliament remains powerless.

It is to this essentially remote set of institutions that the United Kingdom's ultimate sovereignty has now devolved. But in addition to the lack of direct control by the electorate, the institutions are rendered even less accountable due to the lack of transparency generated by the way the bureaucracy works, and not least by the extensive use of sub-committees. Moreover, council membership is drawn effectively from the ranks of the executive governments of the various member states. All this strengthens the impression that power is centralised and its workings are remote from the people.

This situation is a cause for considerable constitutional concern. But reform is blocked by political considerations. One obvious solution would be to increase the powers of the European parliament, both by expanding the co-decision procedure and by giving it greater power to initiate legislation. Yet such a move would represent a considerable step down the path of European integration, which has been strenuously resisted by the national assemblies of several member states. It is also questionable whether such a reform would necessarily resolve the democratic dilemma.

In the United Kingdom, the turnout for European elections is less than 34 per cent, and the votes cast generally represent national rather than European interests and issues (and in particular national party support). If the electorate has at best considerable apathy for, and at worst outright distrust of, the deliberations of a European-wide government, the answer must surely lie in allowing important decisions to be made closer to home and giving back some of the power to the national parliaments. Some Eurosceptics argue that this can best be achieved by Britain's withdrawal from the European Union. But there is no need to take this dramatic and potentially devastating step. Many of the concerns can, and should, be met in the framework of subsidiarity. This is convenient jargon for making sure that as many decisions as possible are taken locally, and is just as vital a principle for the future of Europe as it should be here at home.

The political power of the European Union is the question most frequently debated by the media and national politicians. By contrast, the legal implications of the European Union are frequently left out of the limelight. But the impact is nothing short of startling. European law pervades the daily life of British citizens. Many of our employment rights, our working conditions, our health and safety considerations, and competition in the marketplace have been affected by European law. From the control of pornography to the vexed question of Sunday trading, European law has had an impact on the social conditions in which we now live and work. How has this come about?

The starting point is the way in which European law has been made a part of English law. International treaties are not directly part of English law unless they are specifically enacted by parliament. So it was necessary to draft an 'enabling act' to incorporate the Treaty of Rome, which we did through the European Communities Act of 1972. However, its unique feature is that under Section 2(1) it not only incorporates the provisions of the Treaty of Rome, it also provides that 'all such rights, powers, liabilities, obligations and restrictions from time to time created or arising by or under the Treaties . . . shall be recognised and available in law and enforced, allowed and followed'. Thus all future European legislation was automatically to become a direct and integral part of English law. When we joined Europe in 1973, we were effectively signing up to acceptance of all European law as it might develop in the future.

But not only is European law to be automatically a part of English law. It is also superior to English law. The common law and indeed even acts of parliament are subservient to it. This had been clear before the United Kingdom joined. As long ago as our first application to join, Lord Kilmuir, who was then lord chancellor, told the House of Lords that prime minister Macmillan's decision to apply for membership of the community involved acceptance of a community 'code which becomes part of the law of each particular state'. A cluster of decisions of the European court confirmed this supremacy. This was recently reaffirmed in 1992 by a decision of our own House of Lords. An act of parliament that was on its face against European law was suspended until its legitimacy had been ruled on by the European court. This was the first time that an act of parliament had been suspended since King James II abused that power and was promptly overthrown in the Glorious Revolution of 1688.

There is another reason why the impact of European law has been so pervasive. It stems from the continental legal systems from which it evolved. The approach of this 'civil' law, which differs from the traditional approach of our common law, is to look not to the letter but to the spirit of the legislation. This broad approach to interpretation means that a loosely worded document, such as the Treaty of Rome, can be applied in a wide-ranging way by the judges to achieve its aims. Where the driving force of the European Union is the deepening of unity between the peoples of the individual nations, it is hardly surprising that the European court tends to give effect to this aim. As a result it is seen as centralist.

In the same way, the court is able to draw on what are described as the 'fundamental principles of law'. These are derived from the laws of the member states and they include equality, legal certainty, the fulfilment of legitimate expectations and proportionality. We have to recognise that this approach gives a good deal of scope for flexibility in developing law.

The role of the European court has been a topic of furious debate. Perhaps the most formidable diatribe against it was that of Sir Patrick Neill QC, who sees the court as over-expansionist and undermining the sovereignty of the member states. The finest riposte to this is that of Lord Howe of Aberavon QC, who has looked at milestones in the court's history. He has shown that most judgments have been highly beneficial to Britain's economic and business interests. The direct effects of European competition law have done much more to deter non-competitive business cartels and monopoly abuses than could ever have been achieved by individual countries. The court has also set standards for non-discrimination in employment rights which echo fundamental human rights.

But important issues about the role of the court remain unresolved. What Lord Denning once described as the incoming tide of European law has recently become a flood. We all accept that the European court must work within the framework set up by the Treaty of Rome. But just what are the limits of that framework? Are they workable? And will the judges be sensitive to the need for judicial restraint? Judges are there to interpret law. It is for politicians, who are accountable to the people, to have the responsibility for making the law.

Turning finally to the economic union, a free trade area was relatively easy to establish by removing national customs barriers. But the establishment of a genuinely common market was far more difficult. Progress was almost non-existent prior to the Single European Act of 1986. This adopted qualified majority voting, that is where questions in Europe can be decided by a majority of member states and not vetoed by any single member. This was done with the consent of Mrs Thatcher's government as it was rightly seen as fundamental to driving through the economic reforms needed to increase competitiveness and create the single market. Qualified majority voting is well understood in this country as a way of deciding criminal cases if a jury cannot reach a unanimous agreement. It enables the criminal law to function in a way which reflects the consensus view while not being vetoed by a small minority. It is the same underlying philosophy which makes majority voting an important element in those areas of European Union activity where it applies. The fleet can sail even though one vessel is reluctant to put to sea.

The next stepping stone in the economic union was the Maastricht Treaty of 1991. With its clear aim of creating currency union, it has been the backcloth to the strident debate in this country over the last few years about our place in the European Union. Many think, as I do, that the topic has climbed too quickly up the league table of key European issues. Enlargement of the European Union to the east, the freeing up of labour and social charges, the reform of the common agricultural policy, the completion of the single market and the protection of our environment can all be cogently said to be more important. The competitiveness of Europe is key for all our countries and all our jobs in a fiercely competitive global marketplace. The world markets are a remorseless discipline.

But this is hardly the point. We cannot, as some seem to think, simply 'talk away' the single currency. For the plain fact is that our continental partners have chosen to make the single currency a major priority. It has become for them the touchstone for the development of the Union. We have supported their aim by signing the Maastricht Treaty, albeit with an opt-out for ourselves. To achieve this aim we have all agreed to accept a clear and demanding economic discipline. Member states have set out to achieve what are called the convergence criteria. These require the convergence of interest rates and inflation rates, as well as stable exchange rates, public sector borrowing requirements of less than 3 per cent, and a total of public debt of less than 60 per cent of gross domestic product.

Why do so many of our partners think a single currency worthwhile? At a basic level I have no doubt that they see it as underpinning the political unity and stability of Europe. That certainly underlies the thinking of Europe's most remarkable statesman, Helmut Kohl. For him, and others, it is part of the political priority of deepening the unity of Europe. This aim is backed by more specific economic arguments. It will reduce the cost of buying or selling goods across borders, since the costs of converting one currency into another will not arise. Nor will there be a risk that one currency will fall in value relative to another. It will be possible to compare prices instantly and effortlessly. This transparency will enable customers to buy the cheapest goods, and sellers to attract customers with keen prices. Low inflation and interest rates are likely to be the results of a single monetary policy. The euro should become the third great currency in world markets, alongside the dollar and the yen. There will be greater liquidity in the marketplace, the cost of capital will be lower, and investment will be promoted. The European economy as a whole will be strengthened. It is, they would say, absurd and inefficient for Europe to have twenty or so centres of monetary policy.

This is a pretty formidable raft of advantages. What then are the doubts? There is a concern that monetary policy will become a blunt instrument and that a single interest rate will rarely be appropriate for all countries within the European Union. The loss of the ability to adjust exchange rates means a loss of flexibility, preventing individual countries from adapting their economies to outside events which affect each of them differently. With high unemployment in parts of Europe, inadequate mobility of labour and some inflexible labour structures, regional unemployment and wealth variations may become greater. The European Central Bank will be wholly independent, and may not be sufficiently sensitive to opinion in different parts of Europe. The need to maintain strict economic disciplines once monetary union is established may create tensions which are simply too much for some countries. These tensions are particularly acute at a time of high unemployment in Germany and France, and were reflected in the 1997 French elections. So it is not surprising that, whether or not monetary union may be intrinsically desirable, many here argue that it is premature. They also argue that our economic cycles are out of sync with those of continental Europe, and that the UK economy is more sensitive to short-term interest rate movements. The Eurosceptics add, and they may well be right to do so, that it will be simply one step down the road leading to later demands for fiscal harmonisation. So they say we should draw a line in the sand now.

It is not surprising that there should be these conflicting arguments. The creation of a single currency between hundreds of millions of people, across a number of separate countries, is a novel venture. No one can be at all certain that it will succeed. Nor is there extensive support among the peoples of all our partner countries. Some two-thirds of Germans are said to be doubtful about submerging the mark, which has been the symbol of their economic success, into a wider European currency. In France I recently heard it said that the attitude of their parliamentarians was similar to the resignation of early Christians before being propelled into contests with the lions in the Roman arena. But for the most part the governing political and the business classes in those countries are determined to achieve monetary union on time.

Will it happen on time in 1999? It will be a close call. A good deal will depend on growth this year in Germany and France and whether they can progress the restructuring of labour markets. Unemployment in Germany, and unwillingness there and in France to accept stringent economic reform, could derail the process. If it does, then a short and reluctantly agreed delay might be inevitable. For us in the United Kingdom, the position has not been formally settled. In reality the chances of us joining in 1999 must now be nil. It would need cabinet agreement that entry would be good for this country, the passing of an act of parliament providing for a referendum, and a positive vote in the referendum. The current government is lukewarm, indicating in its manifesto that there were 'formidable arguments' against.

So it is unlikely that we will be in at the start of currency union. There is a strong argument for a 'wait-and-see' approach, for us using our opt-out and seeing whether the euro becomes a durable, hard currency. If it does so, the dangers of staying out could be considerable. There could be risks to overseas investment in this country, which would not arise if we became members. There might or might not be discrimination against the dominance of the City of London as Europe's principal financial market, but there would be no such risks if we went in. Sterling on the outside will be potentially more volatile, prey to the attention of speculators, and we would undoubtedly carry the burden of higher long-term interest rates. Businesses will suffer exchange costs. The price of our goods will be less transparent than if we were part of the single currency, and so potentially less competitive. It will be less easy for our multi-national businesses to grow and join cross-border mergers. Our citizens, who between them made thirty-four million visits to continental Europe last year, would have all the inconvenience and costs involved in their personal foreign exchange transactions. So the current sceptical mood might change sharply after a few years, and we could once again realise that we are being left behind and that we should hitch our wagon to the single currency train.

But if we do join it will be a momentous constitutional change, a further sharing of sovereignty with our partners in the European Union. This is why I am sure that the issue has to be decided by referendum. Not even the most successful single currency will be all smooth going. Tensions will arise, possibly between individual countries. It would be no use joining without the emphatic support of the people so that we can clearly be satisfied that we are there for the long haul. It is one of the most important decisions we have ever faced.

The new government has promised that we will not join without a referendum.

The implications of deciding to join a single currency are far-reaching. For the countries which take this step will move further over time towards economic harmonisation. We should realise that currency union will not be an end. It is not a question of joining EMU and saying that now we have done so the line in the sand can be drawn. We should only join if we are really willing to influence and share in the further economic developments which will follow. EMU is not a self-standing issue, which if completed would end the quest of our partners for integration. This highlights that the ongoing debate on the single currency is not just about that complex and technical economic issue alone. Rather it is part of a wider battle as to how much, if at all, our future lies with the European Union.

When we first applied to join more than thirty years ago, we seemed to understand that the development of Europe must be political as well as economic. After all, the introductory paragraph of the Treaty of Rome speaks of a determination 'to lay the foundations of an ever-closer union among the peoples of Europe'. Some now say that we were misled, and that they did not appreciate that Europe was to be much more than a free trade area. This is unconvincing because the political as well as economic nature of the Union was flagged pretty clearly. But what can certainly be said is that at the time it may have been hard to appreciate how decisively our partners would drive forward to ever fuller integration. There has always been something of a geological fault-line between our island approach and that of our mainland partners. We have mostly been reluctant Europeans looking principally for trading opportunities, whereas they positively believe in the desirability of deepening European union. They, for different reasons of history, see that as in the interests of their own countries. Take, as one example, the view of the Spanish writer, José Ortega: 'Spain is the problem,

Europe is the solution.' They are keen to strengthen the ties between their countries, whereas we are increasingly unenthusiastic about doing so. To those like me who believe that the creation of the European Union is the most positive development of my adult lifetime, this growing gap is sad. I agree with John Major and the last government when they said in a white paper on Europe:

> The United Kingdom's role as a leading member of the European Union is vital to our national interest. ... The removal of barriers to trade provided a powerful trade stimulus which has increased British prosperity and competitiveness. ... The European Union is the basis on which we must consolidate democracy and prosperity across the whole of Europe. In other words it is more than a free trade area.

In short, the Union is good for the whole of Europe, and a strong Europe is in our national interest. We cannot damage this position by being curmudgeonly, or hectoring our neighbours, or muttering like Dylan Thomas' old men who stood in the pub and 'drank to the failure of the dance'. I also believe, as that clear-sighted statesman, Lee Kuan Yew, now senior minister of Singapore, once put it to me, that there is only one attitude for the United Kingdom to take to Europe – that is to be 'in there pitching'. Why?

Firstly, I do not believe that we should ever forget the benefit of stability and the prevention of war which was the original purpose for the creation of the European Community. It would be a bold historian of Europe who would dare to make the assumption that without union armed conflict would be unthinkable. The break-up of Yugoslavia and the Bosnian conflict make this plain. The European Union could not agree on decisive intervention, but the flare-up in the Balkans did not this time drag in other countries on opposite sides. The conflagration was contained.

Secondly, the world is becoming ever more global. Instantaneous communication, the ability to trade and deal across frontiers, free movement of capital, all mean that it is unreal to talk of local parliamentary sovereignty over our economic interests. This country can no more determine in isolation a desired exchange rate, or an optimum interest rate, or a rate of economic growth than Canute could defy the ocean. World market forces play a dominant role. The United Kingdom is not an insular economy.

Thirdly, issues of terrorism, co-operation against crime, upholding of laws, and security and foreign affairs cannot simply be handled by a medium-sized nation state on its own.

Fourthly, we are deeply involved economically with Europe. Our trade with Europe – a market of 370 million people – has grown to almost 60 per cent of our total exports of goods. More British goods are now bought in Germany than in the whole of the United States – and more in the Netherlands than in the six Asian 'tiger' nations and China, Indonesia and the Philippines put together. So we have an immense stake in the future success of Europe, in shaping its development and in reinforcing the single market.

Finally, it is hard, perhaps impossible, to see any sensible alternative. The Commonwealth is now a very loose grouping. Some still fantasise about an Atlantic alliance, but United States politicians remind us that they need to deal with Europe, and that our influence with them will come largely from our influence in Europe.

So we need our place in Europe. Yet this does not mean that we have to become blindly centralist, submerging our distinct culture and attitudes under a relentless drive for harmonisation. Can a balance not be struck? Can the European Union accommodate the differing ambitions of its members? Or are the differences too great?

We are not alone in these concerns about centralism. They are shared in France and Germany as well as elsewhere. No longer do any of their leaders call for a United States of Europe. Nor is this surprising, since these countries, too, have their own distinct national histories, traditions and cultures.

When President Chirac was in London recently, he was asked about the role of the nation-states. His response was that the institutions in Brussels were far from popular in France, that they were seen to have overused their powers, and that power should be devolved wherever possible to the lowest level at which it could sensibly be exercised. Similarly in Germany, Chancellor Kohl recognises the importance of regionalism. Indeed the dissolution of the Soviet Union and the fragmentation of countries in Central Europe are an ever-present reminder that it is a powerful and growing force. So, too, is the German constitution. This entrenches the power of the individual *Länder* as distinct from that of the federal government and it protects these powers through the constitutional court. Germans, too, are proud of cultural diversity. The French and Germans also appear to recognise that problems of low growth, high unemployment and social charges have to be tackled at a national level.

In the jargon of Europe, this search for the balance between central and local decision-taking has been characterised as 'subsidiarity'. In ordinary language, subsidiarity means that decisions should be taken at the lowest sensible level. So the European Union at the centre should only do what is either necessary, or highly desirable, to be done centrally. At Maastricht, the Treaty of Rome was amended to state that:

> In areas which do not fall within its exclusive competence, the Community shall take action, in accordance with the principle of subsidiarity, only if and so far as the objectives of the proposed action cannot be sufficiently achieved by the Member States and can therefore by reason of the scale or effects of the proposed action, be better achieved by the Community.

This is a vital and welcome step in the right direction, but at the moment it lacks clarity and certainty. There is no authoritative guidance as to which areas are within the 'exclusive competence' of the community. So vague and discretionary is the concept that it is doubtful that a court can use it to give protection against over-zealous intrusion into national affairs. Subsidiarity as defined in the treaty is an elusive and slippery concept: Lord Wedderburn has described it as possessing 'feline inscrutability and political subtlety'.

The final cause for concern is that it is far from clear who will police the requirement for subsidiarity in practice. Both the commission and the European parliament have promised to consider it carefully before passing new legislation. And while some former members of the European court have declared it to be non-justiciable, others have expressed the view that the principle is 'amenable to judicial review' and stated that it will have an important role to play in future European judgments. But as we have seen, these are the very institutions whose powers are being sought to be curtailed: *quis custodiet ipsos custodes?* or, who will guard over the guardians themselves?

So at present subsidiarity amounts to little more than a statement of good intention. To operate as a constitutional safeguard much more needs to be done. The United Kingdom successfully proposed in the round of negotiations leading to the Treaty of Amsterdam a protocol which should strengthen its application. It is much needed.

There may well be scope for an even firmer entrenchment of subsidiarity. Some constitutions, such as those of the United States and Australia, provide that the powers not specifically given to the central institutions are reserved to the individual states. The Tenth Amendment to the United States constitution declares: 'The powers not delegated to the United States by the Constitution, nor prohibited by it to the States, are reserved to the States respectively, or to the people.' An unambiguous assertion of this kind could help to prevent creeping federalism, clip the wings of the European commission and protect the wishes of national governments and peoples to take their own decisions on all issues except those which can only be tackled at Community level. In this way many issues – such as the directive telling people how many hours they can work – can be left to the national level. It is not as if the individual countries were uncommitted to fundamental human rights, or unaccountable to a demanding electorate.

Subsidiarity is, in my view, a must if this country's relationship with Europe is to hold. But on its own it will probably not be enough. For increasingly the European menu is including dishes which are not to our taste. Some are pressing for an ever-deepening approach on issues such as immigration, border controls, asylum and security. By contrast, the prevailing instinct in this country is not to integrate our actions on these other issues. In some areas we are already less integrated than our partners. This country is not part of the Schengen agreement on border controls, and we have the right to opt out of currency union. There is debate at the moment as to the extent to which different groupings in Europe should be prepared to move in different directions or at different speeds. This is not an easy debate, but some measure of flexibility of both direction and speed must be accepted if the fleet is to hold together.

Subsidiarity can make sure that Europe only takes decisions which cannot be taken locally. But what of those decisions which will still have to be taken in Europe? These decisions are by definition highly important, and will become even more important to the countries which share a single currency. If we are to trust these decisions to Europe we must be sure that the European Union is thoroughly democratic.

Abraham Lincoln, in his address at Gettysburg in 1863, spoke of the freedom which could only be achieved by 'government of the people, by the people, for the people'. Europe in the twentieth and twenty-first centuries must equally be committed to government of the people, by the people and for the people. But it still has a long way to go. The Union does not seem to speak to the European people and their concerns. And the people feel, quite rightly, that they have little influence or voice in Union matters. The proceedings of the council of ministers take place in private, with frequent settlement of issues by horse-trading. The commission produces documents which are unintelligible to most citizens. The European Court of Justice delivers judgments in lifeless prose. And the European parliament seems remote, limited in its powers and not particularly effective. It is hardly surprising that turnout at the European parliament elections has been so low throughout Europe. Few of us, I suspect, know who our MEP is, and fewer how to contact him or her.

Some steps have been taken along the road to introducing democracy and accountability into the Union and its parliament. So, since 1979, we have direct elections to the parliament, and the parliament has, since Maastricht, had some limited say in the making of European laws. But still, forty years after the Treaty of Rome, the European parliament cannot makes laws on its own. Its powers are limited to seeking to influence the shape of laws proposed elsewhere.

In large part this has come about because the governments of the member states have wanted it to be that way. They have wanted to keep the Union under the control of the individual governments and their ministers. And of course those individual governments and ministers are accountable to their voters. But if the European Union is to be trusted by its citizens and to carry authority, the gap between the people and the institutions – often called the democratic deficit – needs to be bridged. Subsidiarity helps because it brings decisions close to people, and flexibility helps to allow the distinct wishes of the different states to be respected. But ultimately the people must believe in Europe if it is to endure. Debate on how the European institutions develop, how they reach out to the people, and how they are accountable is under way at the Inter-Governmental Conference.

So our membership of the Union raises constitutional questions of some considerable concern. In contrast to other European countries with their written constitutions and constitutional courts, in the United Kingdom there is no constitution against which proposed European legislation can be tested. We do not have the ability, as they do in Germany, to look at changes to the law and argue that they would be contrary to settled constitutional arrangements. This gives Germany at very least an ability to put down a marker with the institutions of the European Union before an attempt is made to force through a law that would raise the need for constitutional change.

Without a written constitution we can have no constitutional court. But we do need some institution which can advise on the impact of proposed community legislation on our own law, highlighting the extent of the changes in advance, and indicating which could be properly covered by subsidiarity. How could we do this? One possibility, which I have mentioned before, could be to create a constitutional commission to give clear and non-political partisan constitutional advice. If our basic rights and interests were being championed by such a commission which was separate from government, it might help to influence the debate in Europe on the proper scope and content of European legislation. Such a commission would also serve to alert the electorate in advance of the nature of the changes taking place and their effect. There is no reason why such a commission should not gain respect both in Europe and in this country to help us both to set out our stall and to alert our people to what is going on.

Europe is still a great issue for our times. We can only speculate as to how it will evolve. But whichever way it goes, it will have a decisive influence on the lives of our children and grandchildren. There are very powerful reasons for this country to stay part of Europe, to stay active, constructive and positive in shaping its future. We should realise that the French and the Germans, and our other partners, value our involvement. They respect our parliamentary traditions, our attachment to liberty, our pragmatism, and they are increasingly influenced by what may be described as the Anglo-Saxon attitudes to business. It is from a positive stance that we can best defend our national interests. But at the same time we will need their tolerance, their understanding of the need for maximum subsidiarity, and some flexibility as to which developments we join. Does Europe have the tolerance and the give for this? Or will the elastic be stretched to breaking point? And do we have the will to play a positive role?

The stakes are high. The gap between those in Europe who want a deepening union and those here who wish to put the brakes on is considerable. I hope it will be bridged. For the last forty years the development of the European Union has served our continent well. It has cemented peace. It has contributed to the emergence of democracy in Greece, Portugal and Spain. It has brought increasingly open markets. It has led to broad agreement on sensible macroeconomic management. All this compares wonderfully with the wars and depression of the first half of the century. There is much that we can do better together than as nation-states acting separately. Sovereignty is not a tom-tom for the tribe, but a national asset to be shared where it is in our best interest.

But there must be a constitutional framework which takes account of the need to push power down to the lowest level wherever possible and to involve the people as real participants. This need is not only felt in this country. No one wants a Europe which piles layers of bureaucracy on top of each other. Ultimately we are back to exactly the same constitutional issues which face us domestically. We must achieve subsidiarity and we must involve the people. This is no more than obvious common sense. Otherwise European institutions, just like those at home, will wither and perish.

CHAPTER NINE

A BILL OF RIGHTS

Every man who has power is impelled to abuse it.

(Montesquieu, French philosopher)

We have a commitment from the Labour government largely to incorporate the European Convention on Human Rights into our domestic law. This is welcome, but there is one highly important omission. Their proposal stops short of allowing our own judges to strike down legislation which contravenes the convention. To mount a challenge to our laws, our citizens will still have to take their claim to the European Court of Human Rights in Strasbourg. We will continue to decline to trust our own judges fully to uphold what has now become our most important constitutional document.

The case for some form of bill of rights is compelling. Why? Written constitutions are, as we have already discussed, no guarantee of freedoms or individual human rights. Nor is there any driving urge in this country for a wholesale re-shaping of all our constitutional arrangements. This urge normally arises when peoples are faced with some fundamental breakdown in government. It arises at the creation of an independent nation from a former colony, on the change from dictatorship to democracy, or during the overthrow by force of existing forms of government. It is one of the strongest arguments in favour of our unofficial if sometimes unclear and vulnerable constitutional arrangements that they have stood the test of time without such dramatic breakdowns in society. They have provided a framework for our survival in wars and depression and in recent decades for economic progress. We do not need a root-and-branch reshaping of our constitutional liberties.

We rightly pride ourselves in this country on the extent to which we cherish those liberties. To cherish freedom is a deeply ingrained national instinct. In a recent survey, the preservation of individual liberties came out top of people's views on the fundamental values of democracy. Lord Donaldson, a former master of the rolls, put it well in a recent constitutional debate in the House of Lords:

> In this country our approach to human rights is, and always has been, different from that of many others. It is a difference of which I personally am very proud. It lies in the fact that in this country the citizen does not have to identify any right to justify his conduct. He has a total freedom of conduct unless restrained by law; and it is for those who complain of his conduct to identify which law it is which interferes with his freedom. He has no need of a list of freedoms, or rights of freedom. He has them anyway.

But, for all its clarity, is this approach too simplistic? Freedoms in any democratic society have to be limited to take account of the rights of other people. The criminal law places clear limitations on individual action, whether on the freedom to drive after drinking too much, or on the opportunity to offer financial services to the public on a false prospectus. If liberty were unchecked and unconstrained it would be abused. Likewise the civil law holds the competing freedoms of individuals in balance, whether between employer and employee, or over the use which someone may make of their land, or over the care with which we have to drive our cars. As Oliver Wendell Holmes, the great American legal thinker and judge, said: 'The right to swing my fist ends where the other man's nose begins.'

So we have to accept restrictions on our actions out of respect for the freedoms of others. But where does the nose begin? This can only be decided by a recognition of what rights we have, and which of those rights are fundamental.

The traditional approach to liberty was to limit it to 'negative' freedoms. In other words citizens are free to do anything not specifically prohibited by the law. This may possibly have been a reasonable approach in the past when state intervention in the life of the individual was relatively limited. But now the individual comes bumping up against the state in almost every walk of life. Rules and regulations abound and touch almost every human activity. Recognising the need to place limits to protect citizens against oppressive actions of the state, and for the entrenchment of basic liberties, most modern countries have accepted the value of drawing a clear line and marking the boundaries beyond which governments may not step. This is the whole purpose of a bill of rights.

For otherwise an authoritarian government may erode those liberties step by step and without seeking the consent of the people. Nor are we in the United Kingdom immune from this danger. Take some recent examples. In a few brief years under just one home secretary, Michael Howard, the right of silence of an accused was interfered with, an attempt was made to centralise the control of the police, a proposal to allow police forces to authorise their own bugging and burgling of private property was almost driven through, and the discretion of the judges to perform their historic function of making punishment appropriate to the crime and the criminal was curtailed. Moreover there was an attempt to restrict by executive action the compensation for criminal injuries contrary to a more generous scheme which parliament had not long before put into legislation. The 'stop-and-search' legislation was widened in scope and the right of peaceful demonstration was restricted. No doubt all these actions were intended to benefit society. But that highlights even more their dangers. Well-intentioned excesses from one government, claiming the moral high ground and the support of the people, over such a short period show just how frighteningly fragile are our liberties, and how they need much stronger protection.

Nor is it wholly true to say that historically as a country we have turned our back on written constitutional protection and that it is alien to us. To some extent the 'traditional' approach, as painted by Lord Donaldson, is not the whole story. For in the past this country has pioneered the demarcation of fundamental rights. Magna Carta of 1215, the limited Bill of Rights of 1689 and the Habeas Corpus Acts down the decades are prime examples of that innovative spirit. But although we coined the phrase 'Bill of Rights' and successfully exported the concept – to the United States of America, to France, to the Commonwealth and to the United Nations and Strasbourg – the home-grown product has largely withered on the vine. It has become all too simple for people to say that our instinctive dedication to liberty means that we do not need the constitutional protections valued by lesser mortals in less fortunate countries. To do so has in the past suited politicians because bills of rights restrain their powers. But this complacency can no longer serve to protect our people against the juggernaut of the modern state. Nor can it serve as a protection of minorities, and the under-privileged, whose voices are too little heard in our current parliamentary democracy.

The international impetus for the recognition of human rights followed swiftly after the end of the Second World War. Not surprisingly a clamour to recognise fundamental rights followed the shattering of fascist tyranny in 1945 and mirrored the horrors perpetrated by those regimes. The Universal Declaration of Human Rights was passed in 1948. Hot on its heels came the European Convention on Human Rights in 1951. The convention comprises an international bill of rights and provides guarantees of rights which include life; freedom from torture and inhuman or degrading punishment; liberty and security of persons; fair trial; respect for private and family life; and freedom of thought, expression and association. Some of these rights are qualified by exceptions which either recognise the right of the state to preserve public order or prevent the rights being used to infringe the legitimate freedoms of other individuals.

The United Kingdom played a positive role in the birth and shaping of these declarations. We were the very first country to ratify the European convention, and since then have been joined by more than forty others. In 1966 we granted a right of individual petition to the European Commission on Human Rights at Strasbourg. This sets in place a procedure which can bring cases forward for decision by the European Court of Human Rights. The last government accepted that such right of petition should be made permanent.

Yet it is a slow process for our citizens to go to the Strasbourg court. A typical case takes six years from start to finish, and some take up to nine. It is more expensive than pursuing a remedy in our own courts; and can sometimes involve claimants in large costs. But over the years successive governments have persistently refused to enact the convention into our own law. Their obstinate failure to do so would have been admired by those who debated long ago 'how many angels could dance on the point of a pin'. For our courts were already able as a matter of our own jurisprudence to take the treaty into account to a limited extent when construing legislation. This is because it is a well-known rule that wherever possible our own laws should be construed to conform with our international treaty obligations. The courts could also sometimes treat the convention as a backcloth to their approach to the development of the common law, or when being asked to exercise their discretion in a particular case. Finally some of the decisions of the European Court of Justice in Luxembourg which constitute the case law of the European Union take regard of the principles enshrined in the European Convention on Human Rights. So through the back door of acknowledging these European Union decisions, which are part of our own law, the courts can to a considerable extent take account of the convention. All this was very esoteric, and the stuff of complex legal argument. What by contrast the courts could not do was to entertain a claim directly under the convention. This straightforward and more effective step was denied to them. They could ski all over the mountains provided they avoided the piste. Incorporation of the convention will remove these artificialities and free up the landscape.

Over the last twenty years regular attempts were made by private members to introduce the convention into English law. It has been passed several times by the House of Lords, but it has not in the past had government support and so has not got through the House of Commons. When in opposition in the 1970s, Lord Hailsham supported its enactment into our law. The Labour and Liberal Democrat parties have supported incorporation from the vantage point of opposition, and the Labour party has now promised to make most of its provisions part of our own law at long last.

This promise reflects and is consistent with popular support for the incorporation of the European convention into domestic law. This has been shown by repeated opinion poll verdicts which are uniformly and strongly in favour of incorporation of the convention. But the last government fought an obstinate and blinkered rearguard action against these expressions of the popular will.

Why? What were the arguments against? There have obviously been practical considerations. Governments have a traditional reluctance to legislate for any restraints on their powers. There are also always demands on resources and parliamentary time which may have seemed more urgent to both government and public than the creation of a charter of rights. There was, too, probably a feeling that government is better insulated from the effect of Strasbourg judgments if claims cannot be litigated in our own courts. Government could always blame those distant and no doubt benighted foreign judges if it disagreed, and then take its time in amending our law to remedy the breaches. By contrast it is, or used to be until recently, more difficult for the government to criticise our own judges and their decisions have to be acted on more urgently. There are also some anxieties of principle expressed against the bill. Is not our record in preserving freedoms good? By no means wholly, and who can say that it is not capable of improvement? Nor is the purpose of a bill of rights to be seen in a short time-scale. Its essential purpose is to check against abuses of power in a future which extends far beyond the coming years.

But in any event our record shows that we have not always met the high standards to which we aspire. Since the right of petition to Strasbourg was recognised, there have been almost forty important decisions against the United Kingdom to come out of Strasbourg. They range from criticising restrictions on the correspondence of prisoners and their access to legal advice, to the inhuman treatment of suspected terrorists, to judicial birching in the Isle of Man, to interference with the freedom of the press created by a House of Lords decision on the doctrine of contempt of court, to the oppressive operation of the 'closed shop', to inadequate review procedures on the detention of mental patients, and to insufficient protection of personal privacy against telephone tapping by police. Most recently the court has criticised, and in doing so reinforced the arguments of many judges and lawyers in this country, the procedures for reviewing the release procedures for those sentenced for life imprisonment. We currently have the worst track record of all the signatory countries for findings by the court that human rights have been infringed. This is not necessarily because we have the worst record on human rights. It is rather that in most other countries abuses are resolved by the national courts without being packed off to Strasbourg. So one of the consequences of non-incorporation has been the regular public humiliation of being denounced by the European court for infringements of human rights. Moreover, most of the decisions affect minorities, who have no particular parliamentary clout. With more diversity, and more minority groups, a bill of rights and the ability of the judges to protect minorities become of ever greater importance. The judicial task is better and potentially more sensitively discharged at a national rather than an international level.

But surely, say the defenders of the status quo, to incorporate the convention would be to involve the judges in politics. After all, recent history in the United States tends to bear out the comment of Alexis de Tocqueville that 'there is hardly a political question in the United States which does not sooner or later turn into a judicial one'. We must be careful to remember that 'the Supreme Court, like the vines of France, is not for transportation. The soil and climate in which it flourishes are not those of Britain.' Clearly this is a legitimate area of sensitivity. In the past those on the left of politics used to contend that our judiciary had a fundamentally Conservative bias and intervened in politically sensitive issues. This argument is obviously now threadbare, given the record of judges under the last government. Indeed, its most eloquent rebuttal is the recent and increasingly strident criticism of the judges, notably by Michael Howard as the last Conservative home secretary. The chairman of the Conservative party, Dr Mawhinney, went even further and used the platform of the party conference to invite the faithful to write to judges with whose sentences they disagreed.

No one can simply sweep aside fears of an over-intrusive judiciary. There is always a danger that judges will be attracted by their developing role in society, flex their muscles and push out their authority further. Most of them are well aware of this risk. Yet judges do have a very clear constitutional function already in checking on abuses of power. It is their task to see that the executive does not act beyond the powers granted by parliament and that the procedures it adopts to exercise its powers are fair. But they do not regard their job as to review the merits of the decision except in rare cases where the government steps outside the ambit of any sensible use of power. The judges do have a self-denying ordinance. Their training and instincts would enable them to apply restraint to cases under the European convention just as much as they do when deciding the rights of the citizen under judicial review. Indeed, one of the most logical methods of incorporation would be to enable citizens to challenge legislation or government decisions as contrary to the ECHR by use of the same procedural mechanisms as are currently in place for judicial review. This would include the need for any complainant to obtain 'leave' from the court before making his application. Such an initial requirement, which incidentally exists where claims are taken to Strasbourg, is a barrier that has proved an invaluable check against the fears of opening the floodgates in judicial review litigation.

Nor are the judges without experience in these areas. They have developed a considerable track record in adjudicating constitutional claims brought to them, when wearing their other hat as the judicial committee of the Privy Council, and hearing appeals concerning constitutional guarantees in the bills of rights of Commonwealth countries to whom we have granted independence.

Some of the stoutest resistance to the incorporation of the convention came from the last lord chancellor, Lord Mackay of Clashfern. He expressed concerns that this would involve judges in political decisions. But the logic of this was very hard to follow. The balancing of rights and liberties, which is what the convention is all about, has traditionally been a task for judges. It cannot be performed by governments, since they cannot be both advocate and judge in determining the extent to which the freedoms of individuals should be limited. In any event we already accept that foreign judges, those in Strasbourg drawn from a variety of countries, may pass judgment as to whether our government has breached the convention. We respect these judgments, and we change our law accordingly. We may complain about individual decisions of the court, as in the case of the shooting of the Gibraltar terrorists, but we do not for a moment suggest that the court is meddling in politics. If we acknowledge that these are judicial issues in Europe, it is hard to see why they cease to be so if the judges are our own judges sitting this side of Eurotunnel. Why do we have more confidence in foreign judges than in our own judges?

Lord Mackay had a fall-back position. He argued that he feared that it would increase the prospect that our judges could no longer be appointed by the prime minister, on the advice of the lord chancellor, because of the greater political sensitivity of the appointment. Would we, he asked, need to have a parliamentary scrutiny process of the appointment of judges in the way that they do in the United States? No one, he correctly asserted, who followed the Clarence Thomas farrago or the hearings affecting Judge Robert Bork, would lightly go down this road.

But this, too, is not a real difficulty. There are other ways of ensuring independence in judicial appointments. One is very simple: the creation of an independent appointments commission. Successive lord chancellors since the war have shown an impeccable record of objectivity, and of disregard for political sympathies, in making appointments to the bench. Lord Mackay's own appointments and recommendations were of the highest quality. Nor are the decisions made on whim or from political bias. The consultation process which is gone through informally has become much more systematic over the years and candidates for the judiciary have generally been tested by acting temporarily as deputy judges or recorders. Immense care is taken to choose judges solely on ability, temperament and fitness for the job. It would not be difficult, as a recent JUSTICE report has recommended, to build on this informal system so as to create an advisory committee which would recommend judicial appointments to the lord chancellor. The composition of this committee would obviously need to be sufficiently apolitical to ensure that a fear of the government taking perceived political sympathies of potential judges into account when making appointments would not materialise. The new lord chancellor, Lord Irvine of Lairg, has taken a prompt and welcome decision to set up an independent body to advise him on the appointment of judges. So, provided this body is constituted in a way which gives proper protection against politicised appointments, another argument against incorporation of the convention has bitten the dust.

So the case for incorporation is very strong. But the government proposes to incorporate it only in part. Legislation will be exempt. The government will be required to inform the lord chancellor and the speaker if proposed legislation infringes the convention. The proposed Human Rights Commission will also be required to advise. All this lessens the scope for government to be indifferent to our rights. It is a marked advance. But what is missing is the ability of a citizen to challenge laws, whether deliberately passed in conflict with the convention or in a case where it is claimed the government legislated mistakenly. When practising at the Bar I defended the government at Strasbourg against claims that shipbuilding and aircraft nationalisation, and leasehold enfranchisement legislation, were contrary to the convention. Cases of this kind would still in future have to be heard in that same court before judges from over forty different countries.

One might ask what the purpose of incorporating the convention into our law is if our courts will still have to uphold laws which conflict with the basic human rights in the convention. The partial approach will give our citizens some extra protection, for instance against administrative and executive decisions of the government – but it will leave them unprotected at home against past or future laws which conflict with the principles of the convention. This is the approach taken in New Zealand, which has presumably influenced the present government's proposal. There the Bill of Rights of 1990 provides that the courts must try to interpret and apply other laws in a way which is consistent with the rights in the bill, but that if there is no way of reconciling the bill with past or future laws then the other law stands and must be applied. Anne Owers, the highly able director of JUSTICE, got to the heart of the dilemma this posed when she said that such a partial approach proposed by the government 'seems to put the courts in a double bind. They have wherever possible to interpret the law as being compatible with the convention, but they can't strike it down if it isn't.'

In Hong Kong the position, at any rate prior to reverting to Chinese rule, was somewhat better. There the Bill of Rights overruled any past laws which were inconsistent. But this still left open the danger that inconsistent future laws could be passed.

Any half-hearted approach is difficult to justify. How can parliament commit itself to the basic human rights in the convention and, in the very same legislative breath, say that any laws which have already been passed, or which may in the future be passed, are immune?

The right approach is surely that taken by Canada. The Canadian Charter of Rights overrides any inconsistent past legislation, and all future legislation unless the future legislation states that it applies notwithstanding the principles in the Charter of Rights. This does not restrict the sovereignty of future legislators, but it does require them to acknowledge that they intend deliberately to ignore the Charter of Rights if they want to pass legislation which is inconsistent with it. This avoids any accidental infringement of rights, and it makes it, in practice, more difficult for the rights to be deliberately disregarded. Parliament would have to be persuaded to pass legislation in the full knowledge that it breached con-stitutional rights. This would be, as it ought to be, a powerful deterrent.

United States judges, German judges and Australian judges can all decide constitutional questions. There is no novelty in giving our judiciary the power under our constitution to uphold to the fullest extent the European Convention on Human Rights. To prevent challenges to legislation would considerably emasculate a bill of rights. We should, having at last taken a positive approach to incorporation of the convention, do so wholeheartedly. There is a safety valve. Even the die-hards may take comfort from recognising that the European convention, when it becomes part of our law, will not be entrenched against repeal by a later act of parliament. True it is that it is rightly hard to repeal a well-regarded, written protection of our rights. Lord Denning said, commenting on the enactment of the Treaty of Rome into English law: 'But legal theory does not always march alongside political reality. . . . Freedom once given cannot be taken away.'

So in practice repeal will be difficult, as indeed it should be for laws which are concerned to protect minorities. But, in the unlikely event that those who trot out the old chestnuts on which resistance is based were proved right, we could always have second thoughts. I do not believe we will. We have a thirty-year history of these claims being decided by the European Court of Human Rights. Principles have been laid down in the case law. One of these principles is that a court is cautious before interfering with a government decision on the ground that it contravenes the convention. It gives substantial discretion, called in the jargon a 'margin of appreciation', to the governments of the individual countries. Only if those countries step clearly outside the boundaries of fundamental freedoms will the court interfere. I believe that in time the arguments against incorporation would, if we were to be bold enough to incorporate the convention to the full, be left stranded on the further shores of history alongside the doctrines of the flatness of the earth and the divine right of kings.

We need entrenched freedoms, and the European convention is an obvious route to achieve considerable protection. It is high time we patriated what has in effect now become part of our constitution. It is time to give our citizens access to our own judges to enforce their rights. Otherwise we place a fetter on their access to justice. It is now almost 800 years ago that we enunciated in Magna Carta the principle that justice delayed is justice denied. It is very welcome that we are to make some progress. But let us do so whole-heartedly and give our citizens protection in their own courts from laws which infringe the convention. Otherwise we simply emphasise that a government which commands a majority in parliament can override our constitution.

CHAPTER TEN

ECONOMIC RIGHTS

> To offer political rights, or safeguards against intervention by
> the State, to men who are half-naked, illiterate, underfed and
> diseased, is to mock their condition.
>
> *(Sir Isaiah Berlin,* Two Concepts of Liberty, *1959)*

For most people in the world poverty and economic and
social deprivation are much more real concerns than
the risk of arbitrary arrest, a knock at the door in the
night or an unfair trial. Yet even passionate protagonists of
human rights shrink from suggesting economic and social
charters. Why? Is it because lawyers and philosophers and
not economists and bankers drive the struggle for human
rights? Is it because it is too daunting to grapple with seem-
ingly overwhelming economic and social need? Or is it
because it is thought that the triumph of capitalism will work
to ensure that living standards become as high as they can be?
Our new government is committed to parliamentary reform.
But none of its proposals seeks to entrench the right to even
basic economic and social rights.

Whatever the reason, constitutional reformers are strangely
coy and cautious when the debate moves to economic rights.
In its recent wide-ranging series 'The British Constitution',
the *Economist* declared that adding social and economic
rights – such as the right to a job, education, medical care,
welfare or protection of the environment – to civil and political rights was, as it put it, 'controversial'. The authors

recognised that such a move might be popular. But they nonetheless felt that in our developed country any attempt to turn access to economic resources into fundamental rights with a higher status than ordinary law 'seems doomed'. To make the attempt, it was argued, would risk the entire concept of a bill of rights. Ferdinand Mount, in his notable work *The British Constitution Now*, was equally doubtful. A campaign for what he called the 'old' human rights – civil and political rights – was quite enough. He took comfort from the belief that respecting civil and political rights changes the whole nature of government so that it cannot help giving birth to economic and social justice.

This approach appears to shrink from the entrenchment of economic rights on the basis that it does not fall within the art of the possible, and might prevent some precious advances of which there is a more realistic prospect. But, more fundamentally, some people shy away from creating economic and social rights on philosophical grounds. They believe that freedom requires the grant of 'negative' or more limited rights and that 'positive' economic and social entitlements are not really rights at all. This controversy has rumbled on down the centuries, and both sides of the argument are brilliantly marshalled by Sir Isaiah Berlin in his essay *Two Concepts of Liberty*. To read his analysis is to realise the sheer complexity of attempts to draw the boundaries of rights and liberties within any society. Those who argue for limited rights do so in the name of freedom. They say that the grant of more positive entitlements would risk an all-controlling, all-pervasive state. It would undermine the enjoyments of the liberties of others, justify large-scale state intervention and downgrade the sharpness of focus needed to secure civil and political rights. Many of them claim that the only true rights are those which do not require positive action to secure compliance. Sir John Laws, a High Court judge, has sought to stress the distinction between these 'negative' rights and those which call for more 'positive' interference. He believes that negative rights, or the right to be left to do as one pleases, are the stuff of constitutions. He argues that by contrast positive rights cannot be made constitutional because they raise issues on which decent and honourable people will disagree. So rights become essentially a rule of minimal interference. The argument goes that moral and legal duties prohibit acts which cause intentional or foreseeable harm. This view regards freedom as the potential right to do as one pleases within a legal framework designed to facilitate the operation of a free market. The outcome of the free market is not seen as having any moral relevance. Nor does it matter that a person's economic position may make this freedom illusory. No doubt some take comfort from the view that the disadvantaged can benefit through the 'trickle-down effect' as wealth enjoyed by the fortunate seeps down to raise the standards of the poor within society. Or perhaps there is simply indifference to whether this happens or not.

This approach, sometimes described as being a radical liberal view, could economically be summed up in Sir Keith Joseph's memorable if harsh observation that 'poverty is not unfreedom'. Freedom is seen as simply the absence of intentional coercion. As Lord Plant, master of St Catherine's College, Oxford, has characterised this view, society is seen as akin to a hotel where anonymous individuals come together to pursue their own individual ends. It is not the job of the hotel management to impose a common purpose on residents. Nor is it their task to redistribute wealth. There is presumably no such group as society. But, if society does not exist, how can it be that limitations are imposed on people's actions – whether to drive under the influence of drink or commit murder – in the interests of the wider grouping in which we live? Presumably the argument is that limitations on freedom of action, such as the creation of a monopoly or the abuse of a dominant market position, are imposed solely to preserve the freedom of other individuals. So would seem to run the argument and, however passionately one disagrees, it is a view held by many of those who can legitimately claim to be true libertarians.

But can this view really be tenable in a civilised country with a mature economy? There are surely some positive rights which decent and honourable people do agree upon. We have long accepted as a society the right of people to have sufficient food to avoid starvation, the right to a free elementary education, to welfare and medical care, and to a basic pension. Should not the duty of the state to provide sustenance to the destitute, which exists under the National Assistance Act of 1948, be an entrenched constitutional safeguard for the hungry and the homeless? Are not these positive rights? If so, as they clearly are, then we have recognised that in a modern civilised society people have entitlements as well as freedoms. At a fiercely practical level, the very impetus of the universal franchise demands that government accepts the needs and seeks to meet people's wants. In a democracy it is only those positive rights which command very broad support which can properly be brought within an entrenched constitutional framework. But that need for consensus, and for caution, should not lead to fear of grasping a challenge because it is too difficult, too far-reaching and controversial. The issues are controversial precisely because they are fundamental to people's lives.

There are many reasons why we should address the challenge now. The last twenty years have seen the triumph of capitalism and the demise of old-fashioned socialism. While different governments will have different priorities, and different emphases, both our major political parties are committed to allowing capitalism to flourish. The separation of 'new' from 'old' Labour, and the whole thrust of their recent successful election campaign, was underpinned by the adoption of many of the economic and social policies of the previous government. The commitment to driving out poverty was stressed, but the main message was to reassure those who had steadily done better in society that they would not be worse off. Elections can be won without the support of the poorest 20 per cent or so within society. The 1997 battle was for the increasingly prosperous middle ground, and not for those who are more marginalised and less likely to exercise their franchise. So the need for a lode-star, a constitutional buttress, under which our society can include all our citizens is of ever-growing importance.

There is, too, a growing realisation or fear that not everything can be left to what Adam Smith described as the unseen hand, which he believed 'would make nearly the same distribution of the necessities of life, which would have been made had the earth been divided equally'. George Soros, an arch-beneficiary of capitalism, recently wrote:

> The cult of success can become a source of instability in an open society, because it can undermine our sense of right and wrong. That is happening in our society today. Our sense of right and wrong is endangered by our preoccupation with success as measured by money. Anything goes, as long as you can get away with it.

Who will say with confidence that he is wrong? For in some advanced capitalist countries, the poorest 10 or 20 per cent of the population appears to be losing out on nearly all fronts. Long-term unemployment is becoming the norm. The living standards of this group are lagging ever further behind. Their educational achievements are inadequate, and their prospects dismally poor. All this in an age when technology is increasingly driving out the need for manual, unskilled tasks. Whole areas can be blighted by deprivation, notably in inner cities. It is hardly surprising that these groups appear to be increasingly alienated from the rest of society. The response to the crime rate cannot simply be to stuff the prisons ever fuller, but must be to create a holistic approach to education, social involvement and, indeed, political participation. We should not assume that fears of a permanent, antagonistic underclass are fanciful. Capitalism exaggerates differences. Between

1979 and 1992 in the United Kingdom the disposable house-hold income of the bottom fifth of the population fell from 10 to 6 per cent of the national cake, while that of the top quintile rose from 35 to 43 per cent. We cannot claim to be a civilised society as we enter the next millennium if we forget the plight of disadvantaged groups. Not least among those are the elderly, who are living longer and forming a greater proportion of our society, but many of whom lack the private pensions or savings to protect them in any degree of comfort against the increasing gap between their income and their long-term needs.

The need of people, and not least the more disadvantaged, for services in their local community is crucial. Yet the increasing deregulation of business, and focus on competition, means that many businesses cannot commercially provide services in areas where a shop, or a bank, or a garage, cannot make an acceptable return. No more can businesses 'cross-subsidise' from a sense of social duty. They are in a remorseless marketplace. The spiralling outcome is that less favoured areas become ever more deprived. This in turn raises the already existing keenness of developers to build on greenfield sites which, as the Council for the Preservation of Rural England has so convincingly pointed out, will diminish the qualities of countryside in our overcrowded island and lead to the increasing creation of inner-city 'ghettos'. Planning policies are beginning to recognise this, with a greater emphasis on the need for redevelopment of existing urban areas rather than further moves out of town. But it is still projected that about 40 per cent of the new development needed between now and 2020 will take place on greenfield sites. There are other environmental issues such as air pollution and road-building schemes which require us to confront competing interests but which are nonetheless fundamental to the society in which our descendants will live.

Obviously we cannot have an economic and social charter which resolves all these issues. We have in the past understandably thought that they should be tackled as individual problems. They are complex and require precise focus and rigorous cost-benefit analysis. But is it nonetheless topsy-turvy that human rights should march on without the inclusion of the economic and social needs which touch people most? For most of the world poverty and misery are the greatest source of oppression. In 1991 the United Nations reported that over 1 billion people, or slightly under 20 per cent of the population of our planet, lived in absolute poverty; 1.5 billion people are deprived of primary health care; about 1 billion adults cannot read or write. Over 100 million children of primary school age do not go to school at all. It is not surprising that against this background some international leaders believe that economic progress is far more important than other human rights. Present-day China is the prime example. In Malaysia, the prime minister Dr Mahathir, under whose government the economy has undoubtedly prospered, has criticised western countries for attempting to impose their values on Asian countries. He has stressed the importance of trade as the real liberator of nations: 'The Cold War was not won by western diplomats or generals. It was won by the workers of the west with their Chevvies and Plymouths, and it was won by well-stocked supermarkets and shopping malls.'

World-wide telecommunications ensure that knowledge of this progress spreads everywhere. Personal freedom, according to Dr Mahathir, should not rank above social harmony. This is a timely reminder that in the developing nations our own emphasis on civil and political rights does not always have the same primary importance. For them growth, and economic and social progress, must come first. Society must accept the non-libertarian disciplines which make this possible. Lee Kuan Yew, under whose dynamic leadership Singapore passed in thirty years from the third world to rank among the developed nations, although educationally imbued with the values of an English-trained barrister, would probably take the same view.

Nor have these countries been the first to stress the fundamental importance of economic development. In 1941 and at the height of his power, President Roosevelt actually nominated freedom from want as one of the four freedoms that should characterise the future world order. He spelled out the vision in his 1944 State of the Union address:

> We have come to a clear realisation of the fact that true individual freedom cannot exist without security and independence. 'Necessitous men are not free men.' People who are out of a job are the stuff of which dictatorships are made. In our days these economic truths have become accepted as self-evident.

Only two years later his words found echoes when the United Nations adopted the International Labour Organisation, a survivor of the old League of Nations. It became a specialised agency which aimed to promote these fundamental principles:

- Labour is not a commodity.
- Freedom of expression and association are essential to sustain progress.
- Poverty anywhere creates a danger to prosperity everywhere.
- The war against want needs to be carried on with unrelenting vigour within each nation, and by continuous and concerted international effort.

The ILO took on a range of obligations which were breathtaking in their sweep. Its task was and remains to promote policies which achieve full employment and raise standards of living, to develop policies on hours and conditions of work which will bring a minimum living wage, to promote a just share of the fruits of progress to all. The right to collective bargaining, social security measures, comprehensive medical care, child welfare and maternity protection, proper nutrition, housing, and facilities for the recreation of culture are all within its mandate. So, too, is equality of education and vocational opportunity. No fewer than 173 countries are now committed to these principles as a treaty obligation. The United Kingdom is one of them.

The last half-century has undoubtedly seen a greater realisation, although still only a partial one, of these aims than any previous period of history. This has been one of the benign achievements of our age. What is hard to tell is the extent to which the aims and statements of the ILO simply foretold the political developments which were to come, or whether they positively contributed to their achievement. A persuasive case can be argued that its existence, its charter and its testing of the actions of individual countries have helped to inform, to underpin, to shape and to raise economic and social rights. So, although it is perhaps not well known, this country has for many years committed itself to compliance with a charter containing the very rights which constitutional reformers are coy of incorporating into our own law.

But that is only part of the picture. For we have also ratified another treaty on economic and social rights, the European Social Charter of 1961. This is not to be confused with the controversial and often much misrepresented Social Chapter of the European Union. The Social Charter is a treaty between the members of the Council of Europe, which was the first of the regional groupings of states set up after the Second World War. The constitution of the Council of Europe states that its aim 'is to achieve a greater unity between its members for the purposes of safeguarding and realising the ideals and principles which are their common heritage and facilitating their economic and social progress'. The council now has almost forty member states. Its institutions, including the European Court of Human Rights, monitor compliance with the European Convention on Human Rights, which is for some countries, including our own, the most important constitutional guarantee of basic rights.

The European Social Charter has economic aims which mirror and build on those of the ILO. They are not legal rights which can be enforced by individuals. But the progress of the member nations is monitored. Over the years the influence of the Council of Europe in this area has been neither great nor prominently publicised. But now that members of the former eastern bloc have joined, it is increasingly seen as a yardstick to measure the performance of countries in protecting and enhancing economic and social rights.

The monitoring process has from time to time led to adverse findings against the United Kingdom. We have been criticised for failing to see that workers and their families receive fair remuneration. Wages that are lower than two-thirds of the national average for a particular state do not meet what is described as the 'decency threshold', unless social security and other benefits raise the standard of living to an acceptable level. But even as late as 1990 the standards of 25 per cent of all workers, and fully 50 per cent of all female workers, in the United Kingdom were found to be below this 'decency threshold'. This and other adverse findings against the United Kingdom have received minimum publicity, yet they give a new dimension to the commitment of the new government to legislate for a minimum wage. For the minimum is likely to be set fairly low, and will in most industries have a negligible impact. Where it does raise standards of fairness it would give belated impetus to the Social Charter which we signed so many years ago. The argument that it would reduce the number of jobs, which is in any event doubtful in most industries, seems less cogent when set against the need of employers to run their businesses cost-competitively but while nonetheless paying what a decent society would regard as a minimum living wage.

For good measure, there is yet a third treaty covering economic and social issues to which our country is a party. This is the somewhat cumbersomely named International Covenant on Economic, Social and Cultural Rights (or the ICESCR), entered into in 1966. In many ways this covenant is similar to the European Social Charter, and covers much the same ground. Its preamble states that the rights 'derive from the inherent dignity of the human person', and 'the ideal of free human beings enjoying freedom from fear and want can only be achieved if conditions are created whereby everyone may enjoy his economic, social and cultural rights, as well as his civil and political rights'. These words are heirs to those of President Roosevelt, which in turn echoed the scar of the economic depression between the two world wars.

Why is it that these treaties are so little known in the United Kingdom? Under our law, unlike that of most other countries, international agreements and treaties do not automatically become part of our law, so our citizens cannot enforce them. They become part of our law only if they are incorporated by an act of parliament. This puts us in an unusual and not specially logical position. We sign and ratify treaties because we think the rights they create are desirable. We allow them to be monitored and even, as in the case of the European Convention on Human Rights, the subject of action against our government, but we refuse to incorporate them into our own law. Without being enforceable the impact of these treaties we have subscribed to becomes more muted. This is no doubt why the UN committee responsible for the ICESCR plaintively urged this country in 1994 that 'Appropriate measures should be taken to disseminate information on the rights guaranteed under the covenant to all sectors of society, particularly to judges, civil servants, social workers and members of other professions concerned in its implementation.'

This suggestion has, so far as I am aware, never been acted on. The importance of doing so is far from academic. For the UN went on to express concern about issues of disparity of wages between males and females, low levels of numeracy of United Kingdom workers, the education of children in the care of local authorities, and harassment suffered by tenants in private rented housing. These criticisms passed almost unremarked, and do not seem to have acted as a stimulus to action. What does this mean? Does it reflect ignorance? Or indifference? Or complacency? Or a lingering disdain on the part of government and civil servants for an international organisation to which we subscribe but whose treaties have not become part of our law?

But in all events this trio of treaties tends to make controversy on the European Social Chapter seem rather small beer. Indeed the Treaty of Rome itself, which we have long accepted, already imposes on the European Commission the task of promoting close co-operation between member states in regard to employment, labour law and working conditions, vocational training, social security, health and safety at work, rights of association and collective bargaining. It was under the core articles of the Treaty of Rome that the *dirigiste* 'Working Hours Directive' has been introduced. The Social Chapter seeks to improve the health and safety of workers, working conditions, the information and consultation of workers, equality between men and women with regard to labour market opportunities, as well as seeking the integration into the labour market of those who are at present excluded. All worthy and pretty incontestable aims. So far the two directives relating to the establishment of works councils and the right to paternity leave have been unobjectionable. Indeed in my own company we have found the creation of the works council on a world-wide basis a positive spur to an ever-improving co-operative approach in the relations between management and staff. My own concern about the Social Chapter is simply that it gives power to the European Commission to bring forward legally binding directives in these areas. Not surprisingly, given the record of the commission for bringing in over-prescriptive measures, many of us in industry have been suspicious. Why is this not a candidate for subsidiarity? Why should not the countries of the European Union implement this statement of principle in a way which fits their national situations and cultures? For we already have wide-ranging social and economic obligations under several treaties freely entered into over the last fifty years.

With this background it would not be so unthinkable to have a charter of economic and social rights as part of our own law as a touchstone against which to test individual economic and social measures. Some countries have already gone further to entrench these rights. South Africa may have far to go to achieve its economic aspirations, but people are in no doubt about its constitutional importance. At the Constitutional Convention held to discuss the draft constitution, speaker after speaker called for the inclusion of rights which, even if not capable of immediate delivery, would commit future governments to prioritising the basic needs of the most deprived citizen. As one speaker put it:

> Social and economic rights address the concrete issues of people's lives – how to feed their children, secure shelter, get health care when they are sick and necessary education. Including these rights in the constitution means that they must be considered at all levels of decision-making at all sectors of society. It does not suggest that the problems of poverty and homelessness will be solved overnight or even in a generation, but it does ensure that the values and priorities are in place to make local and national solutions possible.

This view prevailed. Widespread social and economic rights are included in the South African constitution. They may not make an immediate difference, but they are stars by which to navigate and plot society's course. Some apparently say they lessen government freedom of action. But they undoubtedly entrench the priorities of the people.

So, too, the Dutch and Irish constitutions contain a number of statements of economic principle, and the Indian constitution commits the state to seek to promote social and economic progress. But in none of these countries are these provisions justiciable. They are there as aspirations for government, as a reminder of the fundamental tenets of a fair society, and as navigation points to have in mind in their conduct of affairs.

To entrench these rights constitutionally is to see society not as a hotel, where people come and go as anonymous individuals, but as a family, where benefits are shared, and where there is a concern for other members. Is this too unrealistic? Is it requiring the politicians to put on the sandals of the preacher? Rather this reminds us that freedoms are nothing unless there is an opportunity to exercise them. As Lord Plant has cogently said:

> If we believe that being free to do something implies being able to do it and thus having the resources to do it then part of the common good of human freedom would imply a common level of resources and opportunities to seek to secure for all individuals the same sort of liberty.

In this way the outturn of a market economy is the proper topic of moral debate. Moral judgements can underlie decisions as to changes in the taxation system, or changes to welfare and benefits. As Lord Lawson, who was at the heart of the changes often labelled as Thatcherism, has written in his autobiography *The View From No. 11*:

> it is a serious matter certainly if some people find that they can command in the market place such low wages that their standard of living is an affront to decent people in the society in which they live. That they are genuinely doing their best but their level of skill and their level of knowledge is such that they can't command any more.

In other words, it is a moral issue. This does not mean we can impose one set of moral standards on all our people. But it does mean that where there is a consensus as to fairness and decency we can adopt the principles of the long-standing international treaties to which our country is a party.

We have as a society long accepted that there should be legislation on economic and social affairs. The Poor Laws were an early example in Elizabethan times, as was the Statute of Monopolies early in the seventeenth century. We now have a raft of legislation with economic consequences. From legislation against child labour, laws outlawing sexual and racial discrimination, protecting against restrictive trade practices, providing for rights on redundancy and on unfair dismissal, for unemployment benefit, for income support for those on lowest incomes, for housing benefit, for pensions, and for many others. This does not just reflect morality, or contemporary social philosophy, but it also reflects the reality of the ballot box. It is no coincidence that these rights have largely been created across the first century in which the franchise has become universal. The accountability to the voter helps to ensure that society's ideas of what is fundamentally fair and decent are given expression. But this healthy discipline of the electorate is not on its own enough. What about those at the margins of society who are largely disenfranchised? What about the choices which have to be made as to what we finance through public spending in the future? There is a considerable unresolved tension between the unwillingness of the tax-payer to accept higher taxes and the need for public spending in areas of health, education and social security. There is a relentless demand for ever-rising standards in health, education and pensions. The public perception of the NHS is that it is underfunded, although spending has increased in real terms. This almost certainly reflects the gap between increased expectation and the willingness of the public to pay. The NHS also faces the challenge of increasingly expensive treatment, and technology, with an ageing population. How can we ensure that the poor and disadvantaged do not fall behind the standards of the more fortunate in education, health and retirement income? It would be complacent to think that we can simply rely on our present, or indeed an improved, democratic process to protect the needy.

Constitutional rights, too, are a valuable test of the validity of change. They obviously have their place in protecting against dramatic, hasty reform. But they can also protect against insidious erosion of rights. The gradual decay of rights can present a challenge to any society which lacks fundamental protected rights. Each incremental alteration may appear to be legally impeccable and, in terms of its impact on basic rights, imperceptible. But as the process of change rolls along it may become very significant. Yet under our current political and legal system it is hard to raise obstacles or objections to this process, provided that each step is procedurally valid. So social security rights can be eroded little by little, as can the availability of legal aid. State pensions fall further and further behind income levels. Without the touchstone of legal principle, without the entrenchment of some fundamental standards, step by step our society may increasingly discriminate against the disadvantaged.

Take as one example homelessness. The housing legislation requiring local authorities to provide shelter for those otherwise homeless does not apply to single people. So there is a persistent core of street homelessness. In recent years many of the homeless have been young people without, or cut off from, family or those released from mental care under the impetus to provide care within the community. Many of these people are ineligible for benefits, cannot find a job because of their lack of fixed accommodation, and contrary to myth do not seek to sleep on the street through choice. The one-third of them who are mentally ill receive no health care in the community in which they are outcasts. Through bad luck, or even bad judgement, they have found themselves at the outer margins of society. Much fine work is done by charities such as Shelter, Centrepoint and Crisis, aimed at providing temporary accommodation and whenever possible helping people to escape permanently from homelessness. The last government became gradually more sensitive to its need to make a contribution. But so far as I am aware no party has yet suggested changing the legislation to guarantee the rights of single people to a roof over their head. The Liberal Democrats have come nearest with a promise in their manifesto for the recent general election to 'end the scandal of people being forced to sleep rough on the streets', but this stopped short of promising a guaranteed right to housing. So the nightly spectacle in London's Strand or near Temple station or at Waterloo casts shame on our capital city as do similar scenes in other towns and cities elsewhere across the country. The homeless are more prone to sickness and early mortality than other people. As we approach the millennium there is a group which still exists which is without homes, without jobs, without easy access to proper medical care, with a reduced expectation of life, and with no support from the state. Can we really say that such basic rights do not need to be covered by a charter?

It may be too much to expect a country which has deep scepticism about a written constitution to entrench a charter for economic and social rights. Those who fear that efforts to do so would merely delay the entrenchment of political and legal rights may be wise. Yet the effect of creating a broad framework of economic and social principle might be ground-breaking without being earth-shattering. The grant of specific rights would generally be decided on by government and parliament. The judges would not become involved in areas of social policy-making. At the most they would act as longstops, able to declare that the decline or absence of a right or its erosion contravened basic human entitlement in a civilised society. Government would still be able to discharge its right-ful role of deciding on priorities. By a limited process of judicial review judges would be able to ensure that, whatever the pressures, we maintain minimum standards which our people are entitled to expect. They discharge this task already in considering individual statutes on, say, social security or income support. They police the boundaries to make sure the government does not step accidentally or deliberately outside the standards of a civilised society. Why should they not fulfil this limited role more generally?

But we could do much without even going as far as that.

In the first place there might be caution about making such economic and social principles directly enforceable. We could follow the approach of South Africa and India and entrench rights without giving individuals opportunities of seeking redress in the courts. This would ensure that government had to test its economic and social measures against the criteria laid down in the various treaties to which we have long been a party. To have as a touchstone a firm appreciation that we have long accepted international obligations to achieve economic and social progress would be a protection for the disadvantaged as well as a force for stability. One essential value of human rights is that they prevent the weakest going to the wall. Unless we protect their economic and social rights, cries of freedom and liberty ring hollow.

CONCLUSION

I repeat . . . that all power is a trust: that we are all accountable
for its exercise; that, from the people, and for the people all
springs and all must exist.

(Benjamin Disraeli, Vivian Grey, *1826)*

Our turbulent century has seen remarkable economic
and social progress. Improving living standards,
educational opportunity, leisure pursuits, communication and medical care have opened vistas undreamed
of a century ago. In this country and many other mature
democracies, although not in much of the third world, it has
been a century which for most people has laid to rest Thomas
Hobbes' assertion that life is 'nasty, brutish and short'. In
contrast to many other successful countries we have achieved
radical change without a dramatic rupture in our constitution
and government. Our institutions have rubbed along without
crisis. But perhaps for this very reason the development of the
way we are governed has gradually but increasingly fallen
behind what is needed to involve people properly in a modern
democracy.

The last long-lived Conservative government was one of
the three most significant peace-time administrations of this
century. Its record rivalled the deep-rooted change in society
achieved first by the Liberal government which took office in
1906 and later by Clement Attlee's 1945 Labour government.
In some ways the achievement of Mrs Thatcher and her

colleagues was more remarkable. For they decisively turned back the tide of what had become an apparently permanent acceptance of a moderately socialist society with extensive state controls and state activity. They created a more open economy where individual ability was less likely to be strangled by bindweed. This required the reduction in the power of the unions, leaving management with the ability and responsibility to develop their companies in a highly competitive world. The word, and principles of, socialism have largely disappeared from political debate. The incoming government has accepted most of the changes which the Conservatives had made over almost twenty years. There is now a wide-ranging consensus that a volatile economy is unacceptable, and that low inflation is the only basis for steady growth.

But this time of radical change saw a somnolent and sometimes indifferent attitude to our constitution. This was not surprising in the early years when energies inevitably had to be directed to the rescuing of our country from what threatened to be terminal decline. What was disappointing was that in its later years the last government remained deeply complacent and naively nostalgic about our constitution. Indeed it appeared oblivious to the value of our institutional safeguards. It showed a total failure to realise that sweeping away the right of silence, giving the police the right to authorise their own bugging, amending the Bill of Rights at a stroke to help one of their MPs or drastically restricting the powers of the judges to pass sentence involved significant constitutional shifts.

We now have an opportunity to embrace constitutional change and help shape the rights of our people for the twenty-first century. Whether we will do so largely depends on the new government. Some of the omens from Labour's time in opposition were unpromising. Its failure in the last parliament to challenge some of the draconian law and order measures suggested a disregard of the libertarian instincts which had traditionally driven so many in the Labour party. But the other side of the coin is a commitment to test the strength of the cries for devolution and proportional representation, to change the composition of the House of Lords and to incorporate the European Convention on Human Rights. It is vital that even wider issues should be addressed if we are to safeguard and enhance the health of our democracy.

Some would argue that the underlying basis of changes to our forms of government should be a written constitution. Only in this way can there be a sea wall to protect our freedoms against strong tides which might otherwise wash over them. Some groups, such as Charter 88, argue a cogent case for such a constitution. But it appears to lack the ground-swell of strong popular support and to be outside the realm of currently practical policies. To attempt the complete overhaul of the engines of government would be an ambitious, lengthy undertaking which might well sink under its own weight. A royal commission would be needed with endless submissions and consultations and with little likelihood of achieving a consensus for the contents of such a constitution. It is only extreme circumstances, such as the creation of a new nation or a total breakdown in the existing forms of government, which give the impetus to agree to radical change. Nor have our constitutional forms served us so badly as to make it impossible to achieve radical and worthwhile change by a package of more limited measures.

Nevertheless there must be an underlying philosophy and purpose to any change. The theme of these essays is that people must have a greater opportunity to participate in decisions which affect them. Without this they become alienated from government, and they have no incentive to explore political issues in depth or take an active part in the political process. Politicians consistently underestimate the intelligence and common-sense of the electorate. This is all the more alarming where a so-called strong government can be elected by a minority of the people and can rule for up to five years without the watchdog of an independent parliament. An elective dictatorship is a threat to a stable and healthy society. It may not often lead, as it did in the case of the poll tax, to riots in the streets. But it does not promote social cohesion and stability. Nor does it promote recognition that citizenship involves obligations as well as rights.

Once the importance of the people and their ability to make judgements when properly informed is recognised, then there are some changes which are each worthwhile and cumulatively make for a sizeable and seamless increase in real democracy.

The starting point of any change must be consideration of the role of parliament. We have what in reality is close to a unicameral legislature. Nothing proposed by the Labour government so far alters this. It is an irony that much of the debate in the House of Lords is of far higher quality than in the House of Commons. But the House of Lords does not even exercise to the full those constitutional powers which it has to delay legislation. The House of Commons, where the chamber is all but deserted for most of the time, generally overrides the views of the House of Lords if the government of the day so decrees. For the House of Commons is not comprised of independently minded men and women who keep a check on the executive. It is dominated in all but exceptional times by the will of the government of the day. Between elections the executive is simply over-mighty.

So the return of power to the people must start with parliament. There are obvious ways in which the House of Commons can work more effectively. The greater use of select committees, proper research and staffing allowances for MPs, wider consultation about proposed legislation, greater recognition that MPs can have a career of considerable stature even if they never hold office, would all help to raise the respect for parliament. But the most fundamental change of all is that people should be given the opportunity to change our electoral system. It is deeply unhealthy that for so many years governments have been elected with a minority of the vote but a very substantial majority in the House of Commons. The vote of most of our people is ineffective in the choice of our government. It can be said that the House of Commons comprises close on 400 'rotten boroughs' – rotten because there is a permanent disenfranchisement of the opposing view since these seats could never, in reality, change hands from one party to the other. It is the voters in the more marginal seats who decide which party comes to power. We live in a democracy where there is only a bare minimum of effective participation granted to people in the great decisions of the day. So the case for some form of electoral change is strong. Those who defend the existing system should be prepared to put it to the will of the people, to give them the opportunity to decide whether they would like a fairer and more representative form of election. It is not enough for them simply to advance the questionable argument that strong government has served us well in the past. In principle what counts is that greater fairness should lead to a better reflection of the wishes of the people. This would give a voice, and some purpose in voting in those seats which currently never change hands.

Whatever the electoral system, we must enhance the role which the House of Lords plays. In the United States and Australia, for example, second chambers elected by different voting systems mean that there are checks preventing single-chamber rule. In those countries there is entrenchment of the participation of members of the second chamber from the various regions. To change our second chamber simply by denying hereditary peers the opportunity to participate would not be enough to create a legitimate second chamber. It would rid us of one anachronism. But its replacement by a wholly appointed body, whose members would often be seen as placemen receiving consolation or retirement prizes from their respective political parties, would not enhance respect for the Lords. At very least we need a mix of some appointed members, with a substantial inclusion of those independent of all political parties, and some elected. The obvious way to elect members who could bring a distinct contribution would be to draw them in either directly from the regions, and regional parliaments, or from a Scottish parliament and Welsh assembly if these are created, and from among those contributing most to local government in their area.

But if we start with change to parliament, the case for constitutional reform cannot end there. Tony Blair's statement that we live in the most centralised state in the civilised world commands echo after echo across this country. Such centralisation has probably been inevitable in a country where central government effectively wields unchecked power between elections. But the case for subsidiarity at home as well as in Europe is a formidable one. We have a system of local government where the quality of people wishing to serve has diminished, where powers have been weakened, where only 40 per cent of the people see it as worthwhile to vote. There are alternatives. Accepting the European charter on local government would create a worthwhile framework and would help revitalise local government. So too would giving back more budgetary powers and greater freedom of action to local communities.

The steps which the last government took in its later years to ensure that people have a greater opportunity to play a part in individual organisations such as schools and hospitals were worth while. We should continue to encourage this participation, but we must link these organisations to the communities they serve. We need to secure the proper accountability of these bodies, which cannot be directly to some minister in Whitehall. We must weave in the relationship of these local bodies with the overall responsibility of the local authority to promote the welfare of their area. People will not participate in local democracy if their local authority lacks significant powers. But nor will they do so unless they understand and have views on what their authority is doing or considering for the future. This renaissance of grass-roots power is not just about the granting of services. It is part and parcel of encouraging people to believe that they are involved in the community, not alien from it, and not helpless pedestrians in the path of a juggernaut state. It is also vital for promoting greater responsibility for us all in the development of our society.

Yet strengthening local government may not be enough on its own. Perhaps if we had set about it earlier, and central government had been swifter to appreciate local needs, the head of steam for devolution would not have built up. But the safety valve is about to blow. Devolution to Scotland or Wales is uncharted territory. No one can say with confidence where it will lead. Clearly it is right to give the Scottish people a referendum so that the case on both sides can be vigorously argued. What is important is that the people of Scotland know what sort of parliament they would be getting and what its constitutional relationship with the United Kingdom should be. The so-called West Lothian issue cannot be a bar to devolution. But the illogicality of Scots members of parliament voting on purely English issues, yet not voting on the same issues in their own country, is a weakness. At very least the number of Scots MPs at Westminster would need to be significantly reduced. Nor can it be assumed that the relatively high spending level currently provided by the central budget to Scotland would be accepted without greater critical scrutiny by some of the areas in England.

There does not appear to be any strong or coherent cry for greater self-government in England. Central government has for years divided the country into administrative regions. But it seems highly doubtful whether the local government in those regions would speedily embrace a similar structure for regional democracy. If they did, then many of the anomalies which spring from devolution would disappear. We could have a structure for regional government which was the same across the United Kingdom, as they do in the United States,

Canada, France and Germany. If this were the wish of the people, it might be the most powerful way of securing stronger devolved local government right across the United Kingdom. But that in turn would either add an extra layer of government or pass power upwards from the current local authority structures. It seems more worthwhile to press for a strengthening of the powers of the existing structure of local councils. These are traditions and institutions on which, if the will were there, we could build strongly.

All of these reforms still do not ensure that the people are consulted on important national issues which arise between elections. Those who govern us have tended to be resistant to referendums. It is a fetter on their power, and runs the risk of undermining the assumption that government knows better than the people it serves. There is also a suspicion that referendums are only called when the government of the day fears taking, or is too divided to take, the decision itself.

A referendum is not a constitutional pariah. It has the immense advantage of enabling a campaign to focus in depth on the single major issue. Politicians can argue their cases across party lines. There are issues about how to choose the topics for a referendum and how questions should be phrased. But these can all be dealt with. With modern forms of communication, and the ever-increasing educational level of the electorate, it is surely time that issues on which they have not expressed a clear choice at a general election should be laid out before them for their view.

None of the choices for our country is as momentous as the extent to which we should deepen or withdraw from our relationship with Europe. The acceptance that we would pool our sovereignty with our European partners in areas covered by the Treaty of Rome was the most important constitutional decision of the last fifty years. But there are those who would withdraw, those who would stand back and cede no more sovereignty, and those who would see our role as continuing to play a key part in developing an even closer European

Union. My own view is that this latter position is the only sensible way in which our medium-sized nation can pursue its interests in a world of large and powerful groupings. One thing is sure, and that is that the issue must be settled. But, equally, if the European Union is itself to succeed in the long term it must be prepared to pass more power to its people. The feeling of people that they are far away from the decision-taking structure, that those in Brussels are meddling in internal affairs and that we are ever further from controlling our destiny must be resolved.

One of the great contributions of Europe to the last twenty years has been its part in the development of human rights. In this country the European Convention on Human Rights has become perhaps our single most important constitutional document. It upholds the basic and fundamental human rights which were so terribly violated during the Second World War. There is a tendency in this country to think that our innate values, our stress on freedom, mean that we do not need the discipline of the convention. Not so. Many cases have gone to the European court at Strasbourg and showed that our own approach needed to be changed. We are confident of our system of law and of our judiciary, but government has been and appears to continue to be unwilling to trust our judges to apply these fundamental rights. Our claim that to no one do we delay or deny right or justice goes back to Magna Carta. Yet we insist that our own people should undergo the delay and extra expense of taking their claims under the convention to Europe. It will be the mark of a more self-confident society, a society more at ease with itself, when we incorporate the convention fully into our own law. Without these safeguards preventing the tyranny of the majority, the United States would never have survived as a single country.

No consideration of human rights can overlook the critical importance of economic and social freedoms. It is a fallacy to suggest that legal and political freedoms are all that a civilised society needs. We have accepted as much in the raft of economic and social legislation in this century, which has contributed greatly to bettering the lives of our citizens. But there is always a danger that by some action or omission a balance might be tilted away from what is a minimum acceptable standard. The claim for a minimum wage, provided that in setting it there is a consciousness of the need to remain competitive, is hardly outrageous. Even less so is the claim of the single homeless to be granted a right to a roof over their head. We need to ensure that the social and economic position of the poorest 20 per cent or so of our population is protected. The threats they face come from brutal and brutalising social and economic conditions – rather than from a lack of 'political' freedoms. While constitutional reformers tend to shy away from this issue as being too sensitive or difficult, surely we should consider the more widespread appreciation and acceptance of those economic and social treaties to which this country has long been party. Perhaps in time we will even go further. Obviously we cannot make judges arbiters of economic and social decisions. This is not their role, and it most emphatically is the role of government. But in time judges could be a constitutional longstop, there to point the way if a government steps right outside the boundaries of executive discretion to infringe the minimum standards which our society accepts.

So increase in the power of the people to influence local and central government is crucial, as is buttressing our basic human rights. But in order to exercise this power and individual freedom people need proper access to information. Some form of freedom of information is an essential tool for a more effective democracy. To strike the balance is not easy. Governments, like every other organisation, need to consider their policy options freely. Imaginative discussion could dry up if, at every stage, even preliminary views were open to the public gaze. But there comes a point where discussion documents or green papers are vital to proper consultation. More important still is the access to factual information. It is a natural tendency of governments and civil servants to be sparing with information. Whether on the sale of arms to Iraq, or the use of pesticides in the Gulf War, or the warnings of BSE or the state of our abattoirs, there is an authoritarian tendency to believe that publication of the facts may be misinterpreted and unduly alarm the public. We need a statute which holds the balance between the need for government to preserve its proper confidences and the right of the public to know facts which may affect their lives.

There is an equally powerful reason why the right of an individual to access to information is important. A hundred years ago the state used to have virtually no knowledge at all about individual citizens. Even the recording of criminal convictions was rudimentary. But now, and at an ever-increasing pace, technology is permitting government to have more information than ever before. The need to ensure that there is a right of access to this data has already been recognised. But the Orwellian reach of the state moves on. As recently as 1997, the Social Security Administration (Fraud) Act provided for data matching to be carried out across government departments. This was with the undoubtedly laudable objective of preventing benefit fraud. But there were concerns about the lack of protection for privacy, and the absence of a statutory code as to the way in which information would be used. In the face of House of Lords pressure, including advice from the Delegated Powers and Deregulation Committee, the government eventually conceded such a code. But all this stresses that we need a broad framework of principle to balance the collection of information against the rights of citizens both to privacy and to know what is said about them. Inaccurate information, or the wrongful use of it, can prejudice our rights whether it be to a mortgage or to social security benefit. The citizen must have the opportunity to know what is said about him, so as to correct it if it is wrong.

Arguments about privacy tend to focus on the role of the press and the rights of individuals to what the French have long recognised as a *droit d'intimité*. There clearly are cases where the press invade privacy to obtain a story. If the efforts of the Press Complaints Commission to police the frontiers were to fail, then in fairness a right of privacy would be needed. But we need to be careful not excessively to muzzle the press. For in a relatively closed democracy the press and investigative journalism are crucial to ensure that the public are informed about important issues. The press can be strident and obtrusive, even brash and abrasive, but there is some remarkably knowledgeable journalism in this country and the media are alert to expose situations which governments would often prefer to conceal. What irritates us has, for the most part, to be the price of free speech. The great American jurist Oliver Wendell Holmes said: 'Free speech is freedom for the speech we loathe.'

So the main need for a right of privacy does not stem from the activities of the media. It comes rather from the ever-advancing technology which enables long-range spying on people's activities. Means of surveillance are growing ever more sophisticated. This has not yet impressed the government that there is a need for a right of privacy. But long-range visual and audio surveillance can now be conducted on every one of us at any time and wherever we may be. The subtlety and efficiency with which this can be done will continue to grow. The whole relationship between the use of technology and the freedom of information needs to be debated so that people's rights to information and private lives can be protected and enhanced. It is welcome that the government is to give effect to the European Union data-protection directive and consult on freedom of information and then introduce legislation. But privacy needs a more wide-ranging protection.

These proposals, from reforming the voting system through the strengthening of local government to referendums, are major issues which would all help to involve the people more deeply in decision-taking and in our democracy. Political parties will remain a vital part of our democracy. To be healthy, those parties must involve their supporters in their own decision-taking. New Labour has conspicuously done so during the last few years, seeking wider involvement in the election of its leaders and consulting on its manifesto. By contrast, the Conservative party has given the impression of being more distant from its followers. It is clearly important not only to the health of the Conservative party but also to democracy that in the future it involves its members in the election of its leaders and the choice of its policies. All political parties must also, like the Liberal Democrats, be increasingly involved at local level if they are to mean anything in a democracy in which local powers are strengthened.

A real and accountable democracy needs to be better informed and guided. Several times in these essays I have referred to the need for a constitutional commission, probably consisting largely of senior members of both Houses of parliament. The role of such a commission would not be in any sense party political. It would be there to advise as to whether proposals for changes of the law raise constitutional issues, and so require specific debate. No longer could the government push through a hasty amendment to the Bill of Rights, self-serving to the interests of one of its supporters, without proper debate. The commission could have a clear role in advising where proposed changes to European law would lead to a significant alteration of our own law, particularly in areas of constitutional importance. This would enable an objective view from this country to be put in Brussels, which would be not dissimilar to the way in which the knowledge of the prospective view of the German constitutional court already operates. The commission could perhaps have a role in deciding which issues warranted a referendum, but should undoubtedly be involved in ensuring that there was a fair procedure for providing people with a good summary of the arguments for and against a particular referendum proposal. This could serve as an anchor against which people could test the arguments advanced in the campaign.

The commission might, too, be granted a role in advising whether proposals relating to local government conformed with the Council of Europe's charter of local government. Perhaps, too, it could express a view as to whether particular legislative proposals conformed with the European Convention on Human Rights. But first the idea of such a commission has to be accepted. I believe that, as a country which because of its lack of a written constitution also lacks a constitutional court, we need some powerful, respected body to advise us on the important issues. No doubt it will be argued that the task would be too big for one commission, or that it would be difficult to secure political neutrality, but all these arguments fall away if there is a will to ensure that our citizens are better informed and advised.

But there is a wider purpose and need. A constitutional commission would help us to approach our constitution, and its reform, in the round. Our constitution is not neatly written down in one document. But its diverse papers and practices are linked in a seamless web. We must not fall into the trap of thinking of our constitution as akin to the National Trust. It does not consist of so many grand historic structures, standing alone in glorious isolation, to be visited and savoured singly over a lifetime, and to be restored and developed piece-meal. Our constitution is a living whole. We must not think that we can tinker with or even amputate one part without considering how this will affect the whole. So we must not think of devolution without at the same time considering its impact on local government or upon the composition and functioning of the House of Commons. Nor should we think about reforming the House of Lords without considering parliament as a whole, and about what we expect from both of its Houses. We certainly should not think solely about abolishing hereditary peerages – however easy a target those peers may be. Nor should we think about fundamental rights without surveying the full range of rights, including economic rights, and without considering the proper role of the judiciary.

A constitutional commission could be charged with surveying the whole picture. It could and should carry out regular (perhaps bi-annual) reviews of our constitution, surveying its weaknesses and the results of reform and marshalling the arguments for and against future reform. In this way our politicians and people could be helped to take a more mature and informed interest. The lack of any form of regular review, or stocktaking, is striking. Most of the great bodies and organisations of our society are the subject of regular, thoughtful and disciplined review. Reports and accounts are produced on most activities. So, for example, the National Trust presents a review of its care and custody of that part of our heritage entrusted to it. But the foundation of our society and of our freedoms which gave us that heritage, and which protects us and our children, escapes regular and disciplined scrutiny. The constitutional commission can fill this vacuum.

It is our citizens, as time and again I have stressed, that these essays are all about. Constitutional reform may be a grandiose phrase. But it has a fiercely practical purpose. All forms of government must evolve to meet the changing needs of society. Their framework creates a backcloth for a government aiming to enhance prosperity and educational, economic and social opportunity. Such opportunity must include the right of people to participate more in their government. It is all too easy to be bleak about our contemporary society. It is right to be concerned where standards of education are too low, about long-term unemployment, about the more fragile nature of family life and about the alienation of the underclass. A society which is fair to all its citizens can be achieved only by a powerful and vibrant democracy, sustained by basic human rights enforceable in a civilised judicial system. The cry for a stakeholder society is not new, nor is it one from which we should shrink. It is a simple plea for the inclusion of all our citizens. It echoes the words of John Donne, dean of St Paul's almost 400 years ago, that no man is an island.

As we approach the next century, with all the unknowns it has in store, the one certainty is that to succeed we need to recognise that government belongs to our people and we must be given greater, much greater, opportunity to play full part. Our people should be allowed far beyond the barricades of old. The current healthy atmosphere of reforming zeal needs to do more than just allow a few welcome but fleeting glimpses through those barricades to the land which lies beyond. For that land properly belongs to us all.

FURTHER READING

I have tried wherever possible to acknowledge references and quotations in the text.

For those who wish to read more widely on constitutional issues, there are a number of books that I have found especially stimulating. Ferdinand Mount's *The British Constitution Now* gives a particularly interesting analysis of how the doctrine of parliamentary supremacy became so firmly embedded in our constitutional thinking. *Accountable to None* by Simon Jenkins vividly traces the way in which governments, acting through parliament, can both transfer power to unaccountable quangos and private organisations and at the same time strengthen the power of central government. Andrew Marr's *Ruling Britannia* is a trenchant and well-expressed account of how government works in practice. John Patten's *Things to Come: The Tories in the 21st Century* is the most thoughtful and forward-looking expression of modern Conservative thinking. The *Economist* continues to be keenly interested in our constitution. It has, over the last few years, been alert to focus on both issues of civil liberties and the need for constitutional change.

In some senses, the most remarkable case for change remains *The Dilemma of Democracy* by Lord Hailsham of St Marylebone. Some twenty years ago Lord Hailsham argued for most of the reforms which have now come on to the agenda. He highlighted with compelling logic and a brilliant phrase – the 'elective dictatorship' – the fundamental weakness which lies at the heart of our democracy and which cries out for reform with even more urgency than when Lord Hailsham first alerted us.

Inevitably there have been books, pamphlets and articles which I have not singled out for special mention, but this is not to ignore or deny their importance and contribution, and my debt to them.